Plus
Insider Secrets Revealed!

THE WORLD'S MOST INFLUENTIAL PUGILIST

PACQUIAO UNDER CROSSFIRE

C.S. Granville

INTERNATIONALLY ACCLAIMED SPEECHWRITER

*"His best articles are jam-packed with meat.
Some articles you'll love; others might infuriate you."*

**PERHAPS THE MOST INSPIRING,
ENTERTAINING YET INTRIGUING BOOK EVER
WRITTEN ABOUT MANNY PACQUIAO**

A CULT CLASSIC

Copyright © 2012 by C.S. Granville

Pacquiao Under Crossfire
The World's Most Influential Pugilist
by C.S. Granville

Printed in the United States of America

ISBN 9781624192364

All rights reserved solely by the author. The author guarantees all contents are original and do not infringe upon the legal rights of any other person or work. No part of this book may be reproduced in any form without the permission of the author. The views expressed in this book are not necessarily those of the publisher.

Unless otherwise indicated, Bible quotations are taken from The American Standard Version of the Bible.

www.xulonpress.com

Review by Xulon Press

This is a very interesting book in a different kind of format that will make readers curious about the subject matter. It is a great tribute to not only the boxing star, but to boxing in general. The author's creative skill makes the book exciting even for people who do not follow boxing or have not been interested in it before seeing this book.

Critical Points

- The combination of articles and original commentary is an atypical format for non-fiction; it gives the book a large amount of differentiation, which is important in setting it apart from the other sports enthusiasm books on the market.
- The author's expertise as a journalist transferred over into his work as an author. Some are not able to do both: write very successful articles and bring concepts together in a full book. The articles and the original content between them fit together extremely well.
- There is a good overview of the boxing world in general. The author does well in explaining the back-story of Pacquiao's successes, as well as giving credit where credit is due to other boxing stars.
- It's good that the author includes text in Pacquiao's native language. He could have simply written the translations, but

when the readers see the actual words as they came out of his mouth, that will make the book even more real for them.

CONTENTS

The Author	xi
About the Author	xiii
Dedication	xv
Acknowledgements	xxi
Preface: The author's fighting spirit	xxvii
Endorsements	xxix
The Birth of Pacmania	35
The Pacman Era	47
Pacquiao achieves historic feat	50
The Naked Truth	55
Pacquiao at the Devil's Golf Course with Mayweather, Jr.	68
Complexity of Pacquiao's words: Are they absolutely reliable?	71
Pacquiao caught in headlights	74
Arum has the prescription	78
No knockdowns, only increasing doubts: Pacquiao's victory	80
Pacquiao vs. Marquez stirs up old anxieties	84
Hatton may just freeze this late Spring	90
UK's most formidable sportswriter predicts Pacman by TKO over Hatton	95
A moment of prediction and a dawn of reflection	99
Bloodless but brutal as Pacman stops Hatton in round 2	101
Contrasting signs: Idealist vs. Realist harking in the world of Pacmania	103
Cotto advised by fellow Puerto Rican to wear eye-patch	107

Less understood neuroscience of boxing:
   the Jetweight Theory of Conservation 110
The Golden Rematch: Pacquiao vs. De la Hoya 114
Pacquiao, a new light to Philippine Congress 119
Pacquiao too elusive for a 'Jetweight Cotto' 124
Raising thoughts over the hills of Las Pulgas 126
Intimations and predictions from Pacquiao circle 130
Watch Cotto tonight morphing into a hopeless Pharaoh' 133
Tectonic shift continues 137
Mayweather, Jr and Pacquiao still indispensable
   to each other's glory 142
Pacman checkmates the Grandmaster 153
5 Margarito misconceptions 157
Top Pay-per-View boxing events as of May 2012 160
Pacquiao's 'Black Pope' in ex-cathedra 165
The Real Excuse: Mayweather, Jr. hates Pacquiao's
   right hand - Arum 167
Pacquiao in the Philippines vs. Pacquiao in the US 170
Battling Mosley-Pacquiao for a better imaging rhetoric 173
Team Pacquiao in disorder with 'Black Pope' 176
Pacquiao 'a work-in-progress', learning the arts
   and wiles - Arum 178
Obama-Pacquiao meeting a chance of diplomacy,
   not mendicancy 180
The Zen of Emmanuel D. Pacquiao: Boxer, Entertainer,
   Actor and Builder of Faith 183
Emmanuel 'Manny-Pacman' D. Pacquiao: The Godfather 187
Pacquiao-Pope Benedict XVI meeting can happen
   anytime - Arum 189
Pacquiao becoming the 'Samson of Old' 191
Bowel movement with live worms 194
Colossal upswing return for Pacquiao-Mayweather fight 197
Pacquiao's privacy under serious scrutiny 201
Pacquiao the enlightened and anointed one 203
Pacquiao chooses higher bid for popularity 207
Prelude to my controversial article: Under Obama,
   America becoming Gomorrah 209

Contents

Biased writers grossly twisted Pacquiao's view
   on same-sex marriage 211
Revealing the new Manny Pacquiao with Pastor Jeric Soriano .. 219
Revealing the new Manny Pacquiao with Brian Livingston 222
Intricacy of Bradley's victory over Pacquiao 230
Pacquiao's top ten secrets of success revealed 233
Pacquiao rises to a higher level, nearly becoming
   like Howard Cosell 237
Conclusion: Pacmanian sect rising, to the glory of 'God'
   in the highest 240
Bigger than big picture 246
'Come Fly With Me' 250

PACQUIAO UNDER CROSSFIRE

A model of wit and wisdom for anyone
who struggles to understand the 21st Century's
icon of the Maharlikans

C.S. Granville

The Author

Exclusive photo Copyright @2000 by PACQUIAO UNDER CROSSFIRE

About the Author

Exclusive photo copyright @ 2012 by **PACQUIAO UNDER CROSSFIRE**
Taken at Ron Hubbard Auditorium, Church of Scientology, April 2000.

C.S. Granville, also known as Countryman Simeon Granville, was born Simeon Granville Tolo Hayag Vergara Ampong at Camp Allere in Salvador, Lanao de Norte of Mindanao, Philippines. He is also the book author of "May Your Name Be Sealed" and "Yahweh, the Faithful One," both will be in the circulation soon. A U.S.-educated with multi-degrees, credentialed journalist and a syndicated political columnist in the U. S., he is noted among boxing aficionados, fans and political thinkers for his challenging insights. He writes for The Western Center for Journalism in the U.S. He has also been an active contributor of Examiner.com and other media outlets. He has written several promotional articles for lawyers, doctors, politicians and institutions. Dozens of his best articles are jam-packed with meat and best regarded as reliable sources for broadcast information and for several broadsheets and internet publications. He is a registered law student by the State Bar of California for Juris Doctorate. He won first place in the International Speech Contest in 2000 which was held at the Ron Hubbard Auditorium in Los Angeles, California. In the same contest (above photo), Atty. Stephen Jones of Los Angeles placed second.

Dedication

Specially dedicated to my great friend - now deceased, Engineer Ronnie Lu, 46, of Time Warner. His genuineness has left an indelible mark on our friendship. He is survived by his wife, Emma, a registered nurse, and daughters Chessa and Melanie.

*To my wife
Mary Jane Molina
and my children*

***Exclusive photo copyright @ 2012 by* PACQUIAO UNDER CROSSFIRE**

*John Allen and Jake Lee
To my parents
Edu and Sally*

Exclusive photo copyright @ 2012 by PACQUIAO UNDER CROSSFIRE

and to my brothers
Aquilles, Christopher and Aido, Jr.
And to my sister-in-laws
Joy, Ronessa and Marife
And to my parent-in-laws
Alfredo Molina, Sr. and Faustina Bonifacio-Molina
brother-in-laws
Alfredo Molina, Jr., Marvin Molina
To my conscientious moral supporters
Uncles Dan Ampong & Vilmo Ampong, Esq.

To
Tiya' Lagring, Tiyo' Beneto, Tiya' Elvie, Tiya' Myrna,
Tiyo' Eddie, Tita Katherine, Tiyo' Orencio, Tiya' Betty, Tiya' Luce,
Tiya' Maria, Mama Nane' and the whole Ampong-Vergara and
Tolo-Hayag clans.

To all my fellow Lumadnons of Jimalalud,
Negros Oriental, Philippines

Most of all, to my Heavenly Father and Creator, for choosing me
to exist on this planet earth and for forgiving me of my sinfulness
and for keeping me in His perpetual saving grace, that which He

has been providing to me ever since, through His Son, Jesus Christ, who is also my Creator, my Lord and my Savior.

ACKNOWLEDGEMENTS

This book embodies my philosophy, experience, fascination in classical and rhetorical writing. This is a product of my day-to-day meditations and interviews with fighters, promoters, aficionados, fans and thinkers in the realm of boxing, entertainment and politics and even in the realm of spirituality. Team Pacquiao, Top Rank Promotions, Golden Boy Promotions and Mayweather Promotions and all are critical to this endeavor.

Exclusive photo copyright @ 2012 by **PACQUIAO UNDER CROSSFIRE**
Taken at Charles Turner Trailhead, Mount Hollywood Hiking Trail in Griffith Park of Los Angeles, California.

I am extremely grateful to Emmanuel "Pacman" Dapidran Pacquiao, the world's most influential pugilist of the early 21st Century, who has been the constant source of ideas and channel of inspiration in this book. Though I am not beholden to his wishes, I have become a fan of his phenomenal fights both inside and outside the ring of madness for more than a decade.

My investigative approach to covering boxing events is void of its power without the grace of Langdon & Flynn Communications' towering beauty, Ceatta Bogataj. I have been a recipient of her unparalleled way of handling logistics and credentialing operations for big events. Her distinct professionalism and thoughtfulness have been gems to my advancements in life. And there's Andy Olson, CEO of Magna Media International, whose fine judgment has helped me obtain media credential privileges. Lee Samuels of Top Rank and Fred Stenburg - publicist of Manny Pacquiao from Stenburg Communications, for giving me media access for all of Top Rank's boxing events.

My ardent readers and critics who have supported me over the years: their ideas, their intellectual combativeness and, most importantly, their questions, have helped to make me a better writer today.

My first ever lovely Professor of the English language at Silliman University, Cristina Taniguchi, and Dr. Arthur Forcier, my world religion professor in the US from Oxford University – UK, for influencing me to value life with their esoteric wisdom. They both continue to amaze me with their respective works of arts and teachings.

My endorsers: Xulon Press, Dr. Ed de la Vega, Atty. Michael Marley, Gareth A. Davies of The Telegraph – London, Lorne Scoggins – writer of Examiner.com and associate pastor of Christian Lighthouse Church in Springdale, Arkansas, Robbie Pangilinan of SportsManila.net and Alex P. Vidal of New Millennium Publications.

Chino Trinidad and Migs Aguana of GMA News and their associates, ABS-CBN and all other media practitioners who rallied behind me during the world's frenzy upon my controversial article, "Pacquiao rejects Obama's twist on Scripture," in the month of May 2012.

Pastor Benjamin del Pozo and Mr. Ben Daguman for their surprise visit at my residence and their words of comfort, encouragement and prayers they shared during my most difficult moments, as previously mentioned. Their visit was historic! Their kind gestures have made me become a more compassionate person today.

Acknowledgements

Jiskco Alvarez for his sincere advice and affirmation of my safety and moral support during the same aforementioned personal crisis of mine.

My friends in the LGBT community who have respected my stance and have remained supportive of my calling.

Uncle Dan Ampong for the unwavering moral support he pours upon me as he examines my published materials and the respective feedback they have stimulated from both critics and fans.

My fellow writers and cohorts who shed light on issues in the boxing community.

My fellow Negrense, Alex Rey Pal - publisher of Dumaguete Metro Post, and also my endorser, for his encouragement, suggestions and intimations crucial to this endeavor.

Cora and Roger Oriel of the Asian Journal Publications and my former colleagues, for the impetus I have had from a decade of working with them and acquiring more insights about the run-through of journalism and the business side of its practice, mainly the advertising component of the enterprise.

My great friend Johnny Pecayo, CEO of Manila-US Times, for leading me into covering boxing events and for opening a sports column with my byline.

Oscar L. Jornacion, Chairman and President of Tri-media Group of Companies, who opened a political column for me under the grace of David Casuco, Editor-in-Chief.

Romeo Borje and Victoria Peralta, my mentors in oratory, who were instrumental in my winning first place in the International Speech Contest in 2000, which was held at the Ron Hubbard Auditorium in Los Angeles, California. They both have also helped me become a better conversationalist.

Modesto "Dong" Secuya, CEO of Philboxing.com and Pacland for posting my articles despite the thought-provoking insights they may have that could infuriate Manny Pacquiao and his myriad of fans.

New York Lawyer and Award-winning sportswriter Thomas Hauser, who has quoted some of my statements a few times in his book(s), for the fine encouragement in the field of writing.

Salven Lagumbay, the first ABC-certified Filipino international judge and editor-in-chief of Philboxing.com, and Edwin Espejo, writer for Asian Correspondent and Chapter Chairman of the National Union of Journalists in the Philippines (NUJP) for South Cotabato, Sarangani and General Santos City, for their gift of friendship and moral support they both have extended to my cause.

Engineer Ronnie Lu (deceased), Dr. Ed de la Vega, Leo Royo, Gina Montana-Royo, Manny Pena, Arniel Calonia Arsolon and Randy de la Torre, for their fine photography and genuine friendship.

Steve Bonifacio, Maria Almita Moleta Bonifacio and Raffy Libarios for the computer technical support.

And to all my friends, both in the media and in the other segments of this world, whose encouragement and criticism have made me a bolder writer.

Ellen Mae Sienes Garbrecht, Girard Garbrecht, Grace Hayag-Pomar, Ronnie Pomar and the whole Pomar family in Culver City, Laura Vergara Alice Ramos-Pacheco, Mila Awkworth, Frieda Karamoy, Auntie Evelyn and Uncle Rick Bonifacio and family, Lou Bonifacio, Ninong Angel and Ninang Esther Arafiles and their clan, Digman Clan, Tom Vicente, Art Medina and his clan, and all the families of the White Memorial Church of the Seventh-Day Adventists and the Central Filipino SDA Church for their unwavering kindness.

Rafael Nevarez, Art Medina, Ben Daguman, Jae del Pozo, Tom Vicente, Rodney Tan, Dino Marconi, Levi Gutierrez, Guillermo "Jimmy" Zuño, Helena Buscema, Brian Livingston, Pex Aves, Sherwin Garcia of St. Vincent Medical Center, Patrick Michael Echevarria, Joferdine Cui, Alfred Arrieta, Dennis Maitim, Gemma Flores-Tamula, Sarah Jane Bona, Gift Tan, Angel Pauline Malapitan, Stella Bess Villaflores-Sarabia, Agustin Solis Villanueva, Randy de la Torre, Philipp Uy, Ismael Udasco, Patrick Echevarria, Chito Katangkatang, Robbie Pangilinan, Alex P. Vidal, Reuben and Mirasol, Agustin, Ronell and Veronica Baylon, Rodel and Michelle San Felipe, Bonifacio Deoso and his clan, Abelardo Maravilla, Tracy Ndiyob, Philip Uy, Ismael Udasco, Mansueto "Manny" Valencia, Don and Gladys Roman, Myra Hernandez, Magnaye Clan, Granada and Garsula clans of Negros Oriental, Francisco Arqueta and all, for their fine encouragement.

Acknowledgements

My spiritual advisers: Benjamin del Pozo, Stephen Jakovac, Vic Arreola, the late Ariel Roxas, Archie Tupas, Joselito Coo, Kevin Morris, Nelson Ornopia, James Dok, Ulysses Carbajal, Alfonso Miguel, Jr., Eliseo Arevalo, Danny Ranchez, Eliseo Aquino, Alfredo Molina, Jr., Baldson Euraoba and Erwin Pajares.

My cousins, relatives, friends and fans and especially to my faithful reader, motivator and top commenter, Manuel Pacheco of Albuquerque, New Mexico.

My parents, Aido, Sr. and Salvacion, and my brothers, Christopher, Aquilles and Aido, Jr., for being there and for me giving measures of comfort when my funds are low.

My wife, Mary Jane, and for my sons, John Allen and Jake Lee, my unchanging inspiration, who had slept in their beds for several nights without my physical touch while I was writing my pieces for this book and while I was thousands of miles away from them on numerous days and nights, covering boxing events and conferences.

To the countless individuals along the way, who have made me what I am today.

Most of all, my Heavenly Father and my ever loving Creator, Lord and Savior, Jesus Christ, for giving me this life that always amazes me, and all the blessings, both temporal and celestial.

I am indebted to you all.

MY FIGHTING SPIRIT

I once thought books tell stories. But that's not quite true. In fact, Manny Pacquiao, the world's most influential pugilist, tells stories and "writes" them in the annals of history. My task has been to convey the inspiration from his stories in richer detail, bolder perspectives, livelier analyses, side bar prophecies and commentary. Through an investigative approach to classical and rhetorical literary writing, in the style that characterizes my fervor, I hope you may find these same stories of him from inside and outside the ring of madness even more meaningful. With my limited knowledge and wisdom in this case, my discernment serves as a lens through which I may gain composure in my writings.

Famous story consultant Christopher Vogler puts it right: "A book goes out like a wave rolling over the surface of the sea. Ideas radiate from the author's mind and collide with other minds, triggering new waves that return to this author. These generate further thoughts and emanations, and so it goes."

The sweeping force of this book, PACQUIAO UNDER CROSSFIRE, has "radiated and is now echoing back interesting challenges and criticisms as well as vibrations" of inspiration as to my passion. To preserve the substantive brand of hell-fire effects, I have excluded in this book my controversial piece on same sex marriage, centering on the Levitical law and affecting Manny Pacquiao, U.S. President Barrack Obama, the LGBT Community and the rest of the media practitioners who took several bites on the issue. The same issue has shaken the world's state of moral confusion and the sins of hypocrisy and, much more, the abuse of the U.S. Constitution which is happening in America's halls of power. But, I have included a piece prelude to that same issue affecting Obama's position and also my rebuttal for "Pacquiao rejects Obama's new twist on Scripture," plus the popular responses written by some famous journalists that helped, in some way, put the attackers to rest.

PACQUIAO UNDER CROSSFIRE is a collection of randomly selected articles I have written with "reports on the waves that have washed back" over Pacquiao under such inspiration. Through these articles I seek to engage the readers who have shared with me their ideas at times bordering on controversies and targeting multiple facets of the human mind for fresher perspectives, however infuriating they may be.

PACQUIAO UNDER CROSSFIRE is an argument in favor of taking Pacquiao seriously, and it is addressed in part, at least, to those who either trivialize or idolize him. It is also an argument addressed to those who thereby miss his dynamic and transforming quality of spiritual and moral grounding at the altar of the Maharlikan nation. It is, nevertheless, an invitation for one to enter into a loving relationship with Jesus Christ, our Creator, Lord and Saviour.

PRAISES FOR C.S. GRANVILLE FROM FELLOW CREDENTIALED JOURNALISTS

"Granville Ampong has opened a new frontier in "sports writing". His unique style, backed up by his passion to be good and yet different, separates him from the pack."

— **Ed de la Vega, Graduate of the University of Southern California School of Dentistry; Restorative, Cosmetic and Sports Dentistry. Part-time boxing writer and photo-journalist; Multi-state licensed boxing & MMA cut-man and maker of custom-designed World Mouthguards**

"Granville Ampong is like a baseball umpire who calls them as he uniquely sees them. If the pitch is down the middle, this writer calls it a strike. If it is high and wide, off the mark, he says so in plain language. Ampong admires the Great Man Pacquiao, yes, but he is no idol worshipper. If you want fluff and rump-kissing, look elsewhere. Ampong serves up his views and observations straight, no chaser. He is always a good, informative read."

— **Michael Marley, Law Offices of Attorney Michael Marley, New York**

"Granville Ampong brings an honesty in his writings on Manny Pacquiao, conqueror of the American heartlands. The author has always seen the Filipino hero with a clarity which says as much

about the writer, as it does the fighter. It is a chapter in history which in later years will be remembered as ground-breaking. These essays will form a part of that history."
— **Gareth A Davies, The Telegraph - London, United Kingdom**

"Granville Ampong's passion and dedication to the sport of boxing are easily recognized in the tone of his work. While the true journalism and pure objectivism that he demonstrates invite both acclaim and criticism, he continues to report the truth, and only the truth, exactly as he sees it."
—**Lorne Scoggins, Fort Smith Boxing Examiner and Associate Pastor of Christian Lighthouse Church in Springdale, Arkansas**

"Granville Ampong's book is a great collection of stories that vividly captivate the man that has become the Philippines' national treasure. His words meant no patronizing, yet he elevated the boxing champ into a high pedestal. He captured snapshots of the People's Champ and transformed them into enthralling narratives. This book is a total knockout!"
— **Robbie Pangilinan, Founder of SportsManila.net**

"Recent books about Manny Pacquiao explore the topic of his life, his real needs, struggles, fears, desires. But it was Granville who ventured into this terrain with his revolutionary book. Now, with the new material from the author that relates the book's classic message to today's struggling professional boxers, PACQUIAO UNDER CROSSFIRE continues to tell the truth. It reveals what every struggling professional boxer needs to know about Manny Pacquiao and his conquests. And what every struggling boxer needs to know about himself. A syndicated columnist at Western Center for Journalism, Granville has written a refreshing and readable account of the complexities of being a celebrity and world champion at the same time. Aside from the vivid examples and lively prose, what makes Granville's book particularly engaging is that the author makes linguistics interesting and usable. This book could be the Rosetta Stone that at last deciphers the misconceptions about

Manny Pacquiao as a politician, actor, world champion rolled into one."

    —**Alex P. Vidal, New Millennium Publication, Philippines**

"Reading Granville Ampong's work is like having a hot cup of coffee with him sitting across you and speaking his mind on issues close to his heart with eclectic inputs not limited to the temporal but also the spiritual realm. He writes as he talks so leafing through the pages of his book is akin to engaging him in good conversation. His works are good material for those seeking to delve deeper into the myriad issues in the world of boxing."

    —**Alex Rey Pal, Dumaguete MetroPost, Philippines**

Filipino journalist Granville Ampong speaks to Pacquiao's mass appeal when he writes, "Pacquiao has been a saving grace for the government. The Philippines is in a state of political chaos and economic meltdown. There are many controversies around the current administration. The masses could have overthrown the government (former Pres. Gloria Macapagal-Arroyo's administration); but each time Manny fights, he calms the situation. When he enters the ring, a truce is declared between guerrillas and the national army and the crime rate all over the Philippines drops to zero." — Thomas Hauser, Esq., Secondsout.com

Photograph Story: On August 27. 2012 at 10: a.m., Army Reserve Lt. Col. Emmanuel Dapidran Pacquiao attended the graduation ceremony as the Guest of Honor of the 700 Philippine Army Reservists Class 02-2012 in Alabel, Sarangani Province, Philippines.
Copyright @ 2012 by PACQUIAO UNDER CROSSFIRE
For Arniel Calonia Arsolon; Caption by Arniel Calonia Arsolon

Team Pacman from Loma Linda and Moneno Valley (from left): Paul Pastor, Harley Troy Elegino, Harley TJ Elegino, Felicito Elegino and Manny Pastor. Taken at the MGM Grand Hotel in Las Vegas, Nevada.
Copyright @ 2012 for PACQUIAO UNDER CROSSFIRE

THE BIRTH OF PACMANIA

SEPTEMBER 11, 2001 – The series of coordinated suicide attacks by Al-Qaeda upon the United States were about to unfold with the sun rising and brilliantly dominating the New York skies. It was not even noon in my Los Angeles neighborhood. And no crescendo morning cry was heard from every conceivable avenue. But, people were just too shocked. Up on the Hollywood hill in Griffith Park of Los Angeles, the skies with sporadic grey clouds over the metropolis seemed empty. Not even a soaring eagle nor a man-made object could be seen over Downtown Los Angeles, except the approaching aircrafts to Los Angeles Airport almost every five minutes until all air operations in the mainland came to a halt.

Oh, yes, for the first time in the last six months, I turned on my television set. And there, on Channel 59, flashed the scenes. The United States of America saw the infamy that changed the landscape of the purported advancement and prestige of the security agencies of this greatest land on earth. There was no telling about the mark of the beast, nor was there any story being told about its image that may bear its name with the headlines on the dailies. 9/11 was all about the force of evil capturing such a moment of pain crossing racial lines and, moreover, stoking the heart of inspiration. The infidels in all their subjections beheld the "glory" upon the destruction of the twin towers of the World Trade Center of New York.

But forget all about the face of evil – referring to such eventful moments – that people saw on that cold-blooded slaughter of thousands, in broad daylight and right in our TV sets. Such evil had already transcended all cultures, all traditions, all epochs, and the objective nature of morality, when that day of infamy hit home as never before.

To almost all of us, the interplay of such unkind force into this land of freedom and opportunity called the United States of America, was neither anticipated nor was it bound for its predictability. It was inexcusable. But, to the privileged intelligences of prophetic revelation, as evidenced in the writings of Ellen G. White, an American Prophetess, it was made known in their own "mental flashes of divine inspiration," so to speak. Formidable scholars of prophecies, namely: Mark Finley of "It is Written", Samuelle Bacchiocci of "Biblical Perspectives", Dough Bachelor of "Amazing Facts" and John Carter of the "Carter Report Ministry", have talked about vision and disposal of foresights.

Despite all the tragedies that came out of the September 11 terrorist attacks in New York and Washington, D.C., there was one distinctive development, specifically in the sport of boxing. For many boxing aficionados and fans, 9/11 promised the continuation of the death knell in the ring of madness. The traumatic pain from 9/11 had gone deep into the core of emptiness.

But for many, that emptiness gave pleasure a reason to fill that vacuum. And something came up, though in an inversely similar, yet oddly entertaining and even intriguing phenomenon. In a less cosmic proportion, Manny Pacquiao dropped his own whirlwind "bombshell" about two months before 9/11 struck fear into the hearts of men and women and children.

Paradoxically, Pacquiao's own "bombshell" became the "gospel" to the disillusioned, discouraged and disenchanted hearts of the Philippines. In fact, Pacquiao's victories in America became good news to the downtrodden and to the oppressed. Barely two weeks after his first victory in the super-bantamweight division, the sweeping charisma and boxing skills of Pacquiao, bearing 121 lbs at 5'5" probably at such time, hit home in this supreme foreign land – yes, in the land of milk and honey terrorizing the super-bantamweight division and thereafter all the way up to the welterweight.

It was essentially obvious that the trail he created manifested the rising culture of Pacmania (originally coined by this writer to refer to the wild proliferation of Pacquiao fanatics) and the revival of the boxing world, specifically in the lower division. Pacquiao's victories over David Diaz, Marco Antonio Barrera, Eric Morales, Juan Manuel Marquez, Oscar de la Hoya, Ricky Hatton, Joshua Clottey, Antonio Margarito, Sugar Shane Mosley and others enthralled the boxing enthusiasts and shocked both the skeptics and the agnostics.

Ironically, the first victim was not an American, and not even from Latin America. It was Lehlohonolo Ledwaba, the IBF Super Bantamweight title-holder from South Africa, whom Pacquiao fought as replacement of challenger Enrique Sanchez at the MGM Grand in Las Vegas, Nevada. From the opening round, Pacquiao fought his way up on a full scale attack in an electrifying, non-stop fashion, dropping Ledwaba in round 2 from a short left to the right upper quadrant of the body. Pacquiao railroaded his opponent from round 1 through 6 with feisty moments and dropping him again by a straight left to the chin with 2:27 left in round 6.

But still, Ledwaba, "the master boxer", chose to continue the fight which brought him on again to take a finishing right hook from Pacquiao which slid on his chin only to explode to his right chest, dropping him again to the canvas with 2:05 left in round 6, and thus the stoppage by TKO. It was an event before 9/11 that signaled the tectonic shift in boxing, a schizophrenic haste that brought increasing attractions in the little men's division as Pacquiao seized the limelight as the new IBF Super Bantamweight Champion. The same limelight that Pacquiao beheld himself in glory landed on the pages of the newsprints and more so spelled out through the lips of self-glorified prophets of boxing, tuning up with praise-building phrases "swarming like bees around a cider mill", thus the birth to the world of Pacmania. The boxing world became alive once more with the impelling force of Pacquiao's encounter with the formidable, topmost celebrity fighter, Oscar de la Hoya – the legendary moneymaker of boxing.

To help you understand my perspective about Pacquiao, let me tell you instead of my fascination and my personal intimation about his counterpart – his idol in fact – De la Hoya. De la Hoya, as never before, understands the true maxim of a champion. He knows what it takes to give his best in the ring to meet the expectations of his boxing fans. But he knows, as well, what it takes to set priorities for his wife and kids. And, really, it is not just about a decision based on how he was brutalized in the ring by Pacquiao on that cold night of December 6, 2008. That is just one thing, though. The other is about his courage to explore the meaning of life once more to the fullest outside the realm of boxing.

I started to follow De la Hoya's trail-blazing career just after my arrival in the United States, during which time Pacquiao was only sixteen and not yet in a professional boxing career until he had his debut against Edmund Ignacio in Mindoro, Philippines on January 25, 1995, which he won by unanimous decision.

Fresh from his Olympic Gold Medal win in Barcelona, De la Hoya fought his first professional entry against Lamar Williams on November 23, 1992 at the Great Western Forum in Inglewood, California, which of course, this writer witnessed together with Mexican friends in the neighborhood. In fact, during De la Hoya's early career, I gained foreknowledge about his prospect in boxing as I was living with a Mexican family in Santa Monica, California. My friend and co-worker, Jose "Motivation"Avila, at the old Pic 'n Save store in Venice, on Rose Avenue and Lincoln Boulevard, invited me to live with his family as I was in the process of moving out of my cousin Grace Pomar's residence, thanks for the fine reception of his siblings, Francisco and Evelyn and the whole clan. I simply wanted to acquire a better perspective about my fire of exploring America in a different cultural setting and for some less restrictive inclinations in my days of youth by way of realizing that deep-seated obsession of being free. I was only seven months shy from being a legal alien in the United Stated States of America. My tourist US Visa was expiring with no resolute chance for renewal. Even then, bypassing the legal requirement to stay and survive, I worked five night-shifts a week at Pic 'n Save and the other two nights as a combined task-doer being a waiter and a bartender at the famous East Wind Café on Washington Boulevard in Marina del Rey. I kept both jobs until

I finally got another at Asian Journal, a US-based Filipino-American publication.

I will never forget the weekends I spent with my newfound family. We, indeed, had lots of fun. I stuck around with them and our neighbors who were members of the Santa Monica Mexican gangsters. Together also with these seeming outlaws, we watched Spanish movies and televised boxing events. I found much respect about Mexican fighters in the likes of Salvador Sanchez, Rubin Olivares and Julio Ceasar Chavez of old. I first got assimilated into the Mexican culture before I delved into the mainstream America.

And, by the way, the Mexican family whom I lived with treated me with so much "amor" and "gusto", that I became a part of their weekend gatherings and yearly fiesta. That was when I got to know how much hatred this same family initially infused and harbored against Oscar de la Hoya when their ever great son of the Aztecs, Julio Cesar Chavez, was demolished by this same Chicano (U.S.-born Mexican) in round 4 on June 6, 1996, not discounting a repeat of the same in round 8 on September 18, 1998. Those events of De la Hoya magnified his superstar popularity, but not yet in the household of La Raza. Conversely, it was then I saw that conversion of hatred sowed among the Chicanos and the old generations of Mexicanos into an impartial reverence for La Raza, penetrating as well the very hearts of mainstream America in a much grander scale: the mythical coronation of the Golden Boy. Thus, De la Hoya's series of victorious fights became a part of our weekend appetizers whenever we watched him fight on pay-per-view. We even went to the point of reviewing the recorded fights over and over again. "Oscar de la Hoya" became a household name. He had somehow helped my former favorite liquor store where I usually bought packs of Budweiser, on the corner of Euclid Street and Arizona Boulevard in Santa Monica, increased its sales revenue each time he fought. His popularity surged to the level that even gang rivalries cruising East Los Angeles, South Central Los Angeles and West Los Angeles plummeted to a much lower intensity as they took pride in their new hero in the name of Golden Boy Oscar de la Hoya.

Nevertheless, "respect" was the magic non-verbal cue to them, at least in their own intimation. True enough, De la Hoya was considered to be the best fighter in the world at any weight, "Pound-for-Pound", during his prime years. A superstar whose popularity transcends boxing, he was the biggest non-heavyweight attraction and moneymaker at the gates, defeating eighteen former world champions, one twice, in the process.

Ardent boxing aficionados and fans should never forget that De la Hoya's road to greatness began on the tough streets of East Los Angeles, California. He once said, "I was a little kid who used to fight a lot on the streets and get beat up, but I liked boxing, so my dad took me to the gym." He started boxing at the age of six and reportedly had 228 amateur fights (223-5). He eventually earned a spot on the 1992 U.S. Olympic team. At the Barcelona 1992 games, De la Hoya became the only U.S. gold medalist. He vowed to win at the Olympics for his mother who died of breast cancer when he was working towards making the Olympic games. He once said, "The most important thing I've done in my life was winning the Olympic gold medal for my mother. Every time I won a fight, it was like telling my mom, 'Here is one for you.' She was my motivation, my biggest fan."

De la Hoya went beyond his ring savage. He formed his own boxing promotion company, Golden Boy Promotions, which has quickly risen to its current status as one of the premier promotional companies in the sport today.

Meanwhile, De la Hoya looks forward to continue to work with hospitals and schools, which takes him up to the highest calling - transforming himself into a catalyst of change for community and all. He has been the pride and joy of the White Memorial Hospital where my wife works as registered nurse, to which he donated a building in the name of his mother, Cecilia Gonzales, who was under its care before she passed away, and some vehicles other than financial contribution.

Rightly so, De la Hoya stands firm on his decision. He is never wrong on refocusing on his ultimate path. His biggest motivation – his wife and kids – are his fresh stimuli making his life much more meaningful than ever. One may recall in October 2001, when De la Hoya married Puerto Rican singer Millie Corretjer in a private ceremony in Puerto Rico, he said, "Ever since I met her, my life has been different. I have what I want." Inadvertently, when De la Hoya's career in boxing went sky high, Millie somehow felt left behind with their two children, Oscar Gabriel de la Hoya and Nina Lauren Ninette de la Hoya, while the greatest man of East Los Angeles, whose bloodline is of the Aztecs, was out training in seclusion for a boxing match.

But the time is now for his family. And, from his distinctive countenance and teary voice, up to his executive bearing as he speaks by the lectern, what I see today is a much-stronger Golden Boy – the real Macho in tuned as La Raza – ready to champion on a new pathway to happiness – full, if not complete, until he got addicted to cocaine and alcohol and had extra-marital affairs, all of which he publicly confessed. In fact, he had graduated from a rehabilitation center in Malibu, California and another three weeks of follow-up thereafter.

Yes, as De la Hoya once said, "there is life after boxing." All these happened just after current Pound-for-pound king Pacquiao clearly dominated De la Hoya and put him in a momentary stupor on the stool after absorbing eight rounds of neuro-vascular paralyzing shots to the body and upstairs, aborting the scheduled twelve rounds of boxing last December 6 at the MGM Grand Arena in Las Vegas, Nevada.

Meanwhile, I was not surprised at the outcome of the "Dream Match". It came to pass as per revelation of the article which I wrote which was published by Manila-US Times, dated December 3, 2008, to which, of course, I offer no consolation nor reservation, to wit; "Pacman's Mighty Fortress, bolstering his aura of invincibility." The same article was criticized by one of my good friends. His reason was plain: "Your article touches too much on religion." I respected his judgment. In fact, I respected the man: He is a brilliant editor in his own right.

But, what fascinated me was that, days before fight night, my friend was verbalizing his own prediction that Pacquiao will face a total demolition at the hands of De la Hoya. He was so loud about it. And then when the outcome turned out to be the opposite, he started editorializing his reception of Pacquiao. He would talk about how close he is to Pacquiao ever since the latter launched his sweeping campaign in boxing in the U.S., intimating even to the point that many thought he is the brother of Pacquiao or that he is "Manny Pacquiao" himself, as a matter of resemblance. What a big change in perspective Pacquiao's aura brings!

But, my said friend was not alone. In fact, many have become converts in the spell of Pacmania. Sure, I am just appalled at the intricacy of the human mind's response, at least in terms of emotional level of these so-called, "sycophants." They claimed objectivity in their judgment based on vital statistics of both fighters but not based on basal metabolic index or the degree of muscle wasting and lessening of muscle tone. Nor were they objective when they talked about the non-therapeutic level of magnesium in the blood, or the neuro-vascular intricacies resulting from less nourishment and much less the simplicity of faith, gifts of power and speed of the other.

In fact, they can flip from side to side anytime. And the same "sycophants" on fight night gambled by thousands for a De la Hoya win. I can attest to that. And these were Filipinos. Very sad, indeed! Fact is, the dehumanizing gruesome prospect of boxing does not dwell in the periphery of one's thinking. But, it transcends to the very life itself of entertainment. The stimulus it generates gives so much pleasure to the superfluous-seeker of pastime. The same stimulus, nevertheless, fills up the emptiness of one in the realm of inspiration, which, in this case, empowers an emotional observer to subconsciously overrule his judgment, if not becloud the same.

That's the mystery of inspiration. Pacquiao somehow drew his discernment to light which, in this case, may have bolstered his aura of invincibility against De la Hoya. He can never separate faith and performance, except when he dispensed his cash for poker and cockfighting games and in some way, probably for what he once called, "manly call" with top-end girls in the entertainment industry of the Philippines. But, aside from his now-abandoned vices, the confluence of his faith and performance in the ring was just amazing to behold.

I do not need to claim having a third eye to discern such transforming influence of Pacquiao to his ever increasing draw from the general public, especially in the Philippines and in the densely populated regions in the US where Filipinos thrive. But, Pacquiao can definitely take courage from the fact that, despite his extravagance in gathering and partying with the elites (politicians, actors and actresses) and his occasional lack of faith, God used him anyway, even mightily. I just hope that Pacquiao is not beholden to these elites as he tries to close the relational gap between the rich and the poor. In fact, that is quite a noble thing for him to do. How can he learn not to let his lapses turn him away from continuing to press on ahead in faith? No one can divine.

Weeks before his fight against De la Hoya, the Manny Pacquiao website campaign centered on "Spread the faith. . ." And so the leading newspapers all throughout the world bore headlines that left no doubt as to the same line of thought from the theme when they landed on their respective news stand, and I quote: "RP idol: Lord, it's You, not me" – Philippine Daily Inquirer dated December 11, 2008; "Pacman's faith from above prevails" – Valley Sun Chronicle dated December 8, 2008; "Pacquiao's faith brings the difference" – Philadelphia Oracles dated December 7, 2008; "Pacquiao's faith spellbinds De la Hoya" – Washington Chronicle dated December 7, 2008.

Then I saw the same sycophants march in high esteem and sing hallelujah to the newly crowned Pound-for-Pound King who clearly lifted the clouds in their minds about prospect of dominating the fight. These same sycophants closed the distance with the king from one corner of the world to another. There, I saw the conversion process, a clear-cut vindication of what had just transpired. Still, I was not surprised, nor dumbfounded.

Yes, Pacquiao convincingly silenced his armchair critics. His fight against De la Hoya was the epitome of the former's boxing career. Whatever one previously called such mega-fight – a farcical or a mismatch – between Pound-for-pound King Manny "Pacman" Pacquiao and Pay-Per-View King Oscar de la Hoya, it surely set the world stage for what could be a crucial moment in the history of boxing. So, the tectonic shift in boxing continued.

But let us not forget that this meritorious fight between these two great men had served as a lens through which we see how the human mind responded to this entertainment stimulus despite the economic turmoil. To understand this is to immediately lift the clouds in our minds about our present condition, especially for the Maharlikan nation, the Philippines, in particular. The Philippines has been in a vacuum for inspiration and for real heroes for many centuries now. What Pacquiao did in the ring of violence has evolved into a romantic interplay between politics and inspiration, religion and lifestyle sophistication.

Whatever condemnation you may have for this man may not fit the aura that the Creative Power of the Universe has given to him, at least for now. He should not adulterate "God's power" in him and in Scripture, to just make himself look good before the public and to hope that such can translate into political votes.

Think of this, for example: In the Scriptures, despite the fact that David of Old was sinning too much, God's power was still in his favor. For one thing, Bathsheba, daughter of Eliam, was first married to Uriah the Hittite, one of David's champions, before she was married to David. After seeing her bathing from his balcony, David had an affair with her and got her with child. After failing to persuade Uriah to go home and lay with his wife, he arranged for Uriah to be slain in battle. And yet, if you are justified by faith in Jesus Christ, you might meet David in heaven considering that David had shown a repentant life in the finality. Such is what Pacquiao now claims as bearer of the Gospel of Jesus Christ. In the case of Pacquiao, his case is yet to be revealed to the fullest at the right time. What could be in store for a man whose heart is-weak but to some degree, is one of gold? And don't tell me he does not have a repentant heart. The utmost Power from above truly cares, especially in the midst of one's despondency. And Pacquiao knows better of his well being, lest he would deceive the many.

Team Pacquiao, somehow, has a stronger groundwork for Pacquiao's security and strategic affairs, most especially in the US. Other than the divisive "Black Pope" as his business adviser in the person of Michael Koncz, his activities outside of the confines of his family may just have been remotely academic. And so the mystery flares up but only to the less informed.

Curious minds must know that no purported hero in the history of the Philippines had ever made it into the hearts of every living

Filipino. But Pacquiao is one of the exceptions. Even my four-year old niece knows who Pacquiao is, at least in her own intimation.

The name "Pacquiao" adds distinction to the lives of the Filipinos, at least in terms of outlook. Inspirations emitting from the life of their post-modern icon has brought out their imprisoned minds from the bondage of economic depravity and debility in the lack of inspiration, to one of optimism and spiritual skepticism to some degree. Rightly so, when we think of "Manny Pacquiao," we think: construction worker, baker, cigarette vendor, philanthropist, the legendary Asian boxer, descendant of Lapu-lapu, Sarangani congressman. In short he is one of the greatest men of the Maharlikan nation. But alongside that list stands another facet which we foremost know: a man of God, so they say.

While it is true that Pacquiao exhibits in his personal story a controversial past, he makes no effort to hide his own failures. Yet, he will always be remembered and respected for his heart of God. And knowing how much more we share in Pacquiao's failures than in his greatness, we should be curious to find out what made him a man after God's heart. He, like David of Old, seems to have an unchangeable belief in the faithful and forgiving nature of God. To many, he is a man who lives with great zest. He sins many times. But, he is quick to confess his sins. In fact, he never takes God's forgiveness lightly or his blessings for granted.

True, Pacquiao stands firm basking in the limelight of giving glory to his Creator, a direct contrast of what De la Hoya gears up into. De la Hoya resorted to making his fight against Pacquiao a personal revenge of what he perceived to be an easy way to avenge the withdrawal of the latter's intent to establish a contract with him. And for De la Hoya, he felt it necessary to demolish Pacquiao in the realm of his own power and strength. What difference a perspective can make!

As to the intricacy of his fight against the Mexican hero, most boxing pundits only saw the physical and boxing skill advantages of De la Hoya. But, Pacquiao saw a mortal man of De la Hoya's stature defying Almighty God. He knew that he would not be alone when he faced De la Hoya, who was perceived to be cocky, in some instances. Because Pacquiao saw this clearly, he fought a good fight of faith and even fought him more effectively, contrary to his detractors' expectation. Criticisms, nonetheless, couldn't stop Pacquiao from attacking De la Hoya at every inconceivable angle in that ring of madness. In fact, he was and still is, unafraid to make his own trail. And, it's nevertheless about the heart of the True Maharlikan from the blood-thirsty aorta of Mindanao versus La Raza from the gang-infested section of East Los Angeles. Pacquiao inevitably built a mobile magnet around him and wherever he goes, he turns a crowd into a frenzy. And so the tectonic shift in boxing bolted to a new era.

Maharlikan icon's wife Maria Geraldine "Jinky" Jamora-Pacquiao, along with friends, joined boxing trainer Boboy Fernandez, in a long, brisk walk toward the peak of Charles Turner Trailhead, Mt. Hollywood Hiking Trail in Griffith Park of Los Angeles, California; Fernandez is Manny Pacquiao's closest childhood friend and has been assisting him in his training since his amateur days. This photo taken on May 28, 2012 during Manny's outdoor training. **Exclusive Copyright@2012 PACQUIAO UNDER CROSSFIRE** *for Engineer Ronnie Lu & family.*

THE PACMAN ERA

*D*ECEMBER 6, 2008 – What seemed to be a tune-up fight by the Pay-Per-View King, Oscar de la Hoya, for Ricky Hatton turned out to be an unprecedented backlash that put the brains of Angelo Dundee, Daniel Zaragoza and Ignacio "Nacho" Beristáin – the Golden Boy's mentors – in the state of vacuum. These three men cannot seem to put the puzzles together to one piece. But, who is the man who can truly unfold the complexity of Pacquiao's strategies?

After getting one-sided, brutal beatings by Pacquiao from round one through round eight, De la Hoya sat on the stool, found himself staring to the center, feeling lonely, no, frustrated and distressed in fact, pondering what might come to pass in the ninth if he won't give up at a such crucial moment – a grisly knockout! He was beaten to a pulp. His left eye swollen shut and peri-orbital turned purple plum. And his face bruised by punches Pacquiao landed, as if from nowhere.

"I had to stop the fight," said Beristáin, noted Mexico City-based boxing trainer and manager and Class of 2006 inductee into the World Boxing Hall of Fame, who is considered by many to be Mexico's top trainer.

"It was the best decision I've ever made for the honor of Oscar." However, "My heart still wants to fight, that's for sure," De la Hoya said. "But when your physical does not respond, what can you do? I have to be smart and make sure I think about my plans."

De la Hoya, who was trained by Freddie Roach in his last big fight a year ago, could not throw punches. Paralyzing shots from Pacquiao's hands put him in a momentary stupor, except for round three in which he showed a bit of his trademark flurry. But, it was not enough to punctuate the said round to his favor.

De la Hoya, nevertheless, looked so old against the style of Pacquiao, whose movements were reminiscent of fighting cocks with breeds of Kelso, the zig-zag lateral sweeper, and Hatch, the voluminous frontal-cutter and buster, crossed. In the mold of Generation X fans, Pacquiao is more than just a character. "If Pacquiao is the "hip-hop" of today, then De la Hoya is the monotonous classical [music] of yesterday," said Jeanette Williams of Las Vegas, one of the boxing fans of Pacquiao.

De la Hoya's precision, indeed, dropped tremendously bearing his being flat-footed and sluggish all throughout the fight. No bouncing observed, in fact. Experiencing a big surprise of Pacquiao's agility and strategic circling movements with vicious, surgical assaults, De la Hoya felt the impact of being disarmed from using his left hooks.

"He can't just pull the trigger," said Freddie Roach, award-winning trainer of Pacquiao. "Taking the left hand away was the key," Roach said. "We took Oscar's left hand away from him and once we did that, the fight was over."

De la Hoya, who was whisked to a local hospital skipping his attendance in the post-fight press conference, did not officially announce his retirement. Never before was he beaten as badly and as cleanly and as decisively until he faced the Filipino phenom. Conversely, the only clear loss he had was when he was knocked out by a perfect shot to the liver by Bernard Hopkins in 2004. All other losses he had were split decisions, inclusive of the Mayweather fight.

Pacquiao, who not only was as elusive as Mayweather, Jr., threw more punches that kept De la Hoya's potential assaults at bay. In fact, Pacquiao was far more impressive against De la Hoya than Mayweather in maneuvering surgical shots. Asked if he wanted to fight Mayweather, Jr., Pacquiao answered with his usual response: "I am just a fighter. It is up to my promoter to decide." At least, that was his usual line, which, to many boxing fans, has now become "a Mickey-Mouse order of the day."

Arum, who still promotes Pacquiao as of this writing, said he wouldn't discuss a potential opponent for Pacquiao until after the holidays (December 2008), but it was clear his bigger fights were yet to come. During those moments of Pacquiao's victory over De la Hoya, lucrative fights already flickered to set up against Ricky Hatton and Mayweather, Jr., if the latter, who had declared his retirement, decided to come back to the ring, which he did precariously.

But, Hatton was seen as the likely next opponent of Pacquiao as was intimated by the HBO Pay-Per-View honchos and co-promoters at such time. Meanwhile, Pacquiao ended the debate as to whether "The Dream Match" was a mismatch or a farcical one as stirred by the media. "The media, the press is never wrong," said Arum. "You all said it was a mismatch and it was a mismatch."

Inclusive of his win over De la Hoya, Pacquiao improved humbly with 48 wins, 3 losses and 2 draws with 36 knockouts. And the tectonic shift in boxing bolted to a new period – the Pacquiao Revolutionary Era – signaling his defiance to the dictates of the World Boxing Council (WBC), whereby Pacquiao superseded the imposition of the WBC President Jose Sulaiman's persistent order to have Pacquiao defend his WBC lightweight title, which he won from David Daiz via TKO in round nine on June 28, 2008, against Juan Manuel Marquez for a trilogy. Pacquiao won over Marquez via a split decision in their second encounter on March 15 the same year at the Mandalay Bay Resort and Casino in Las Vegas, Nevada, however controversial it was. As noted, their May 8, 2004 fight was upheld as draw, probably the most difficult fight that Pacquiao ever had. Will Pacquiao continue to bypass the ranks of WBC's boxing authority?

Pacquiao by far is now symbolic of a new trail, at least not just in boxing, but, to the lives of the Filipinos and to the prompting mindset of modern fighters who have become victims of unfair deals with small purses out of their fights.

Yes, he was and still is the man, in that regard.

PACQUIAO ACHIEVES HISTORIC FEAT

JUNE 28, 2008 – Outside along the strips, transients were relishing the ambience, slowly increasing by the hundreds – then thousands – as the scorching heat of the sun retreated deep to the west. But it had been madness inside the Mandalay Bay Events Center, packed with 8,362 attendees, with everyone screaming – yes, cheering in fact – vis-à-vis chanting Manny! Manny! Manny! and countering Diaz! Diaz! Diaz! Mexico! Mexico! Mexico! Only the credentialed journalists and judges and a few others appeared to be calm, albeit with tachycardia. These included the sixteen players of the Boston Celtics who came to watch the fight.

Then, the bell rang for the main event of the evening. If that sounded benign, no one knew better than Pacquiao. Having been newly crowned World Boxing Council Super Featherweight Champion in 2008, he had a fatal intent to snatch another belt – this time from WBC Lightweight Champion David Diaz en route to his fourth world title, in this fight dubbed "Lethal Combination."

Lethal Combination? Perhaps. But what happened was plain, one-sided, lethal destruction. The dynamic, controlling forces of these two feisty, gutsy and combative individuals brought the grisly attacks and counterattacks into an astonishing halt! Pacquiao (45-3-37 knockouts) scored a bloody, brutal knockout in the 9th round at 2:24 and became the new WBC Lightweight Champion. This was the same category though belonging to a different sanctioning body namely the World Boxing Organization and World Boxing Association, which Flash Elorde failed to capture when he was knocked out by Carlos Ortiz in 1964 at the Rizal Memorial Sports Complex in Manila. Pacquiao's victory sealed his legendary status as the first Asian Boxer to win four titles in four different weight divisions and firmed up his claim as the new pound-4-pound king of the world.

Pacquiao landed a total of 230 punches and 180 power shots versus 90 and 59 respectively by Diaz. Diaz, a rugged southpaw and a tenacious Chicano with a fiery heart, gave it his all as he tried to handle the fast power-punching challenger, which ironically put him as the heavy underdog in their twelve rounds of boxing. Meanwhile, Pacquiao red-rocketed his fight with Diaz in an all-time high. A southpaw by nature, he fire-bombed more than seventy percent of his brilliant hooks to the body and to the head at different angles. Pacquiao's right-hand punches also exposed Diaz to such ferocity, attacking in an assassin-like efficiency and pummeling him until the referee intervened. His lateral movements opened up windows for his debilitating jabs to both Diaz's left and right quadrants of the gastric region.

Even then, Diaz stood his ground and refused to submit his might to the challenger. Defiant, having the blood of "La Raza" painted on his right face in the 6th, he kept his tenacity at pace. But, it was increasingly evident that the law of diminishing returns gave him the clue of a seemingly hopeless case. Punishing power shots kept landing, as if from nowhere.

But, as Pacquiao steam-rolled his foe into submission in the ninth, a crushing left to Diaz's chin sent the brave heart face-first to the mat, failing to defy gravity. He was the same Diaz who was sent to the canvas by Eric Morales during their fight the year before, which he survived and sprang even more mightily to keep his belt. This time around, with Pacquiao, Diaz never moved and never made an effort to get back up and into the match he knew he could not win. His left eye was swollen and turned purple, while his white trunks in the front side turned into a patchy crimson red. Diaz showed a huge heart but delivered no answer to Pacquiao's swarming style.

The Anatomy of the Critical Power Shots

Surgical power shots, which carried so much authority, reduced Diaz into a rookie sparring partner. Blade-like uppercuts caught his nasal bridge leaving a cut in the second round, then another in the right upper orbital and a blow to the left eye which began to swell. Just in the middle of the fifth, profuse bleeding was evident from the right upper orbital area precipitated by an unrelenting onslaught of power shots, so amazing to behold. Pacquiao landed not one, nor two, nor three with his series of combos but five to seven shots to the body and upstairs, peppering Diaz to his last especially in the second and in the eighth. These combinations gave Pacquiao 10 versus 8 for Diaz in both rounds. It was like Pacquiao displaced the viciousness of the recent typhoon "Pepeng," which killed 288 Filipinos in the Philippines, upon Diaz without merciful restraint.

The Stronger Side of the Legend: Without Merciful Restraint?

Probably not true, to some boxing pundits. Pacman brought dignity and genuine sportsmanship into the sport of boxing. In fact, it was the same fighter who approached the referee in the sixth during its time-out and tried to persuade Vic Drakulich, the third man in the ring, if he can stop the fight because of the size of the cut in the lower edge of Diaz's right eyebrow, which was about 5 centimeters in length and profusely bleeding. It was the same Pacquiao who bent his knees and who grabbed the right hand of the fallen son of the Aztecs (being Mexican-blooded and one of the Aztec Indian heritage) in the hope of conveying about how he felt sorry for him, to get back up for comfort measures. While Pacquiao marveled at his talent in boxing, he felt at such a moment the dehumanizing extreme and gruesome prospect of this said sport. Many regarded Pacquiao as a man whose nature invokes a kind and forgiving spirit and a mind unafraid to travel even though the trail may not be marked. And, in fact, only Pacman can truly define his game of life.

Post-Fight Press Conference Notes

I bounced from my ringside seat to the press conference as it proceeded under the watchful eyes of the Las Vegas Police to the ground floor of the Mandalay Events Center. Access was exclusive to Mandalay Bay personnel, VIPs and credentialed journalists. It was stressful carrying my laptop and its accessories and my camera and also a handful of old notes and some clippings of my old articles from previous boxing coverages all in one bag. My shoulder was heavy and a bit sore from the pressure of my twenty-pound black leather Targus. The crowd leading to the conference area was tight as well. But, it was lots of fun. There, at the conference, I sat in the third row from the front, and Robert "Bob" Arum, the Godfather of Top Rank, started officiating the press conference.

At the outset, Arum made a statement as to why this event generated only 8,362 attendees compared to one with Juan Manuel Marquez which yielded 9,100. The reason, according to Arum, was the exorbitant prices of gasoline which he blamed on George W. Bush. In a few moments, former WBC Lightweight Champion David Diaz came to the stage upbeat and jubilant. He intimated in jest: "If you know the license plate of the truck, please let me know." He anticipated fairly the potential reaction by the audience about the extent of damage on his face from Pacquiao's power shots. Diaz dealt the audience with the skill of a toastmaster. Bearing with winning personality, he was nevertheless so appreciative about the support he got from his fans and from Arum who paid him $ 850,000 for the fight.

Diaz exhibited a good sense of humor and wholesome composure. He expressed admiration for Pacquiao's awesome speed but not so much about the power of the latter. In fact, "He is so fuckin' fast. But, I have a great fun even though I lost. Someday we will get it back again. God bless you," said Diaz, who maintained the same humble personality even in the weeks before the fight. I remembered Diaz's kind gesture of granting me an exclusive interview at my favorite pier in Santa Monica, California which lasted ten minutes despite his hectic schedule. That was two months before the fight during his media tour with Pacquiao.

Finally, the new WBC Lightweight Champion came. "I am so happy because I won by knockout. I am so lucky," said Pacquiao, who also felt elated upon knowing of the presence of the Boston Celtics during the fight as he is a Celtics fan. Asked if he expected the win by knockout, he said: "I did not expect that I could win by knockout. I did not expect I could win this fourth world title. Because of you guys, I won the fight."

Pacquiao, who just moved to 135 pounds for this fight, "felt so comfortable, stronger." He said he thought he would rather "stay in the 135- pound division or consider moving up to 140 pounds." The new legendary hero expressed no preference as to who he would fight next at that time. "I am just a fighter. It is up to Bob Arum, my promoter, to choose an opponent to match with me," said Pacquiao who now demonstrated better proficiency in the English language. "But, I will be ready to fight this November (2008)."

THE NAKED TRUTH

The author interviewing Top Rank Godfather and celebrated Harvard lawyer Robert 'Bob' Arum at the famous Biltmore Hotel in Los Angeles, California on January 11, 2011.
Exclusive Copyright@2012 by PACQUIAO UNDER CROSSFIRE
for photojournalist and boxing commentator Leoncio "Leo" Roy, Jr.

*P*acquiao is definitely the world's most influential pugilist today. However, my current assessments with about 85% of the credentialed journalists from mainstream America and Europe think that he can never be more popular today without the flashing name of Floyd Mayweather, Jr. Nonetheless, about 95% of the well-informed boxing fans here in the United States of America, according to the same survey, consider Mayweather, Jr. to be the world's pound-for-pound king of boxing, as of this writing.

But, Mayweather, Jr., in some way, cannot just dismiss his boxing career without fighting Pacquiao. Mayweather's perfect record would just become less than perfect without Pacquiao's price tag. Even though Mayweather, Jr. has the clear upper-hand over Pacquiao in matters of his chance to win and that he has the better hold over the American market, Pacquiao still has the knack to make their fight, if it happens, more thrilling and more heartbreaking. He also has the chance to beat Mayweather, Jr., regardless of the percentage of probability.

Mayweather, Jr. has been regarded as the most accurate puncher and the least hittable fighter bearing 42 undefeated professional fights. But Pacquiao may just be the right fighter who can stamp out that zero off his record even if Pacquiao only has a slim chance and even if the fighting odds favor his style and advances, which this writer believes to be less favorable. Popular demand dictates these two great fighters must face off in the ring of madness. And no doubt, both fighters are indispensable to each other's ultimate glory.

In some sense, Pacquiao might just be too constrained by these confirmations from boxing fans and credentialed journalists, resulting in his contentment with fighting less threatening fighters. Fighting against better-skilled fighters about his age might just be too risky for his political career. For Pacquiao, victories and great performances in the ring translate to political votes. Being a legislator for the 15th Congress of the Philippines, he is gearing up to run for governor in the May 2013 Philippines elections in the province of Sarangani. Pacquiao is also egging for a groundbreaking quest for the highest office in his country a decade from now. And no better speculation circulates than the prospect that he would now use his last two possible fights, one in November and the other in early Spring of 2013, inclusive of his June 9, 2012 fight with Timothy Bradley, to promote his image and to instigate and to refresh favorable national dialogues among the Filipinos all throughout the world. This self-driven manipulative affair with the media can blur the lines of competence with a masterfully created morality play through the ring of madness. And, so they say, Pacquiao himself, void of true academic honor and respectable qualifications for the highest post of Philippines, cares less for true competence as shown by his lack of foundational learning from secondary education, even though "he passed the aptitude test" to qualify him to get a college education.

Meanwhile, back when Mayweather, Jr. took a nineteen-month hiatus from the ring of madness after his fight against Ricky Hatton of England on December 8, 2007, Pacquiao strategically captured the No. 1 spot of the pound-for-pound ranking as soon as he demolished World Boxing Council lightweight titlist David Diaz and an electrolyte-imbalanced, muscle-wasted Oscar de la Hoya, by technical knockout and by referee technical decision respectively, even after that fancy split decision he took up over his longtime nemesis from the Aztecs, Juan Manuel Marquez of Mexico City – all three in 2008.

In that De la Hoya-Pacquiao fight billed as The Dream Match, De La Hoya, who was heavily favored to win the bout due to his size advantage, was expected to be the heavier of the two on fight night. But, Pacquiao weighed 142 pounds and De La Hoya 145 pounds at the official weigh-in before fight date and De La Hoya entered the ring at 147 pounds to Pacquiao's 148.5 pounds. Some of my fellow writers speculated that 147 pounds could have been too far above Pacquiao's natural weight against the larger De La Hoya. Even then, the outcome was one of Pacquiao's defining moments in the history of his boxing trek that solidified the claim of his promoter, Top Rank Godfather Robert "Bob" Arum, of his being the pound-for-pound best boxer in the world.

But Mayweather, Jr.'s come-back fight and easy-win over their common foe Marquez started to blur Pacquiao's distinction as most boxing pundits critically viewed Mayweather, Jr.'s skills and intelligence as far superior to Pacquiao's. Both of Pacquiao's protracted performances and Mayweather, Jr.'s superb one against the best of Marquez have all become the lens through which a clear order for the pound-for-pound ranking will be established, however subjective it may be.

But, the fact remains: Pacquiao fought thrice against Marquez only defeating the Mexican on the judges' scorecards with controversial decisions – a draw in 2004, split decision in 2008 and majority decision in 2011 – the latest being seen by a majority of boxing fans, even by Pacquiao's own people, as "Top Rank's infamous robbery in the fox hill's kingdom". I still cannot help but think that the judges made the wrong decision. One intricacy in judging a boxing match, for sure, is that it is merely a subjective experience and has nothing to do with the skills of the prognostics, wherein they seldom fail. Judges may have less foresight of the potential feedback of the outcome of their decisions, which may not attest to their sagacity as to what boxing fans and critics expect.

Pacquiao's popularity would remain in an open-and-closed parenthesis unless a fight, not in the courts of law, between him and Mayweather, Jr. transpires. Like my colleague who believes that without fighting Mayweather, Jr., I don't think Pacquiao can get more popular in the American market. It's like Pacquiao has lost that crisp of his punches with the mainstream media's realization, as he tries to manipulate the less informed ones into believing, that he is really hungering, not dodging, a Mayweather fight.

Back on March 13, 2010 at the Dallas Cowboys Stadium in Arlington, Texas, I covered Pacquiao's fight against Joshua Clottey and from my ringside seat I witnessed how Pacquiao was having trouble executing a nutcracker approach upon Clottey's "peek-a-boo tank." For twelve rounds, Pacquiao threw 1,231 punches, landing 246 while Clottey landed 108 out of 399, showing the latter a much higher rate of accuracy.

And now, let us tie this up with prospect of a fight between Mayweather, Jr. and Pacquiao. Pacquiao's winning prospect over Mayweather, Jr. must have already dropped significantly, especially at sports betting sites, even if Pacquiao knocks Marquez out in their fourth encounter, possibly before the close of 2012. Sure, more bets would be laid favorably on Mayweather to win. Conversely, Pacquiao would be showing forth fast hands but might just be less accurate of a hunter against Mayweather, Jr.

But Pacquiao would have a better chance of winning against Mayweather, Jr. who is clearly gifted with supersonic hands and feet and ring intelligence than just avoiding such a multi-million dollar fight at the altar of alibis and romancing with his armies of writers and behest of his cohorts and stick-to-less-than-goodness sycophants.

How will Pacquiao weather Mayweather, Jr.'s counter-punching ability that exceeds Marquez's sporadic bombs? Styles make fights, and just by a boxer's style and the complexity of each fighter's arsenals, the outcome would be more of one that is less predictable. But, will Pacquiao be more of an accurate attacker? Consider this: Pacquiao had so much difficulty breaking down Clottey's defense even though the latter was just simply standing right in front of him, void of lateral movements while mounting his own bilateral forearm shell defense. In fact, Clottey was never a moving target. What if Clottey counter-attacked Pacquiao consistently just like he did in round 9 through 11, which had Pacquiao's head snapped thrice or more, and showed a masterstroke of footwork and derring-do such as that of Mayweather, Jr.'s? Would it be any different at all?

Yes, styles make a fight and may rarely duplicate a scenario, so to speak. But, whether Pacquiao really has that distinguishing reach to muster effective attacks against Mayweather, Jr., considering the latter's elastic shoulder-rolling tactic plus quick jabs like that of a Jack-in-the box. This is not even a matter of debate or of mere speculation. For boxing fans, clouds of doubt will have to be lifted once these two fighters get their feet inside the ring of violence, but only if Pacquiao accedes to the wishes of his beneficiaries and boxing fans.

Pacquiao believes he can't go wrong by following Arum's prescription, *no* matter how toxic its side effects would have upon the system of the boxing world, which may have already been causing encephalopathy to the boxing minds. It's like in Pacquiao's world of destiny there has become a one world order. And for Arum, it's the safest order of the era for Pacquiao's complex affairs, which spill over to business, showbiz and politics, however injurious it is to the latter's standing before his rallying, marching sycophants and less informed supporters, en masse.

The fact is, the boxing public may have been too intoxicated with Pacquiao's playing games with Arum over counter-puncher Mayweather, Jr.'s fanfare, especially after his non-convincing victory over Azteca's brilliant counter-puncher, Juan Manuel Marquez in their third encounter. You see, Arum knows Pacquiao is allergic to effective counter-punchers. That's why he has prescribed a remedial intervention based on what he believes as an effective countermeasure to neutralize Mayweather's virulence. That's why Timothy Bradley became the choice for June 9, 2012. And Mayweather, Jr. would be under Arum's isolation protocol, at least in these days before next fall – in November, if not until the early spring of 2013.

I strongly doubt a Pacquiao-Mayweather fight would ever happen, unless Mayweather, Jr. would really look bad in his upcoming fights. One thing though, while Mayweather, Jr. hovered quietly above Pacmania just before his 90-day jail time was reset to begin on June 1, Pacquiao began brandishing his boxing clout with the Philippine media, saying he is "willing to fight Mayweather, Jr. even with a smaller share so long as the fight will happen." And just when Judge Melissa Saragosa of Nevada, on a sweeping powerhold, granted Mayweather, Jr.'s wish to move the starting date of his jail term to June 1, Pacquiao changed his gear as Mayweather, Jr. seized the chance for a May 5 fight. Mayweather, Jr. declared valiantly via his official Twitter account: "Manny Pacquiao, I'm calling you out. Let's fight May 5th and give the world what they want to see. My jail sentence was pushed back because the date was locked in. Step up Punk." Now, Pacquiao wanted not a smaller share but 50-50 split. Worse, he rejected the $40 million fixed offer as guaranteed purse from Mayweather, which may have been his biggest guaranteed purse ever, if he agreed to it. Is Pacquiao now playing games and becoming a non-trustworthy bubbling head?

Even then Pacquiao insists: "Whoever the fans want me to fight, I will face him atop the ring. I don't choose fights. It is my promoter who does because it's his job. My job is to fight, everybody must realize that; I've said this over and over before and I'm saying this again, I want Floyd Mayweather Jr. to be my next opponent and I haven't changed my choice despite recent developments."

If Pacquiao so intends to be sincere in his articulations, then he should not be jumping into the pit of destruction even if Arum says so. But, he even asks Arum 'how high?' Pacquiao may have lost that ascendancy of trustworthiness, even before the national scene of Philippine politics. He learned early on the wiles and ugliness of sliding from what could be called honorable. He has done enough damage to his ever respectable stature, even if the projected mega-fight materializes. Pacquiao has even less appeal with voters by being the elected Philippine legislator who incurred the highest absences and all. Such would be a run-to-hell mockery upon the sanctity and prayers of the 15th Congress of the Philippines. Even then, Pacquiao continues to fool the public: "Whoever says I'm ducking this fighter or that fighter, doesn't know me, or just plainly wants to put me in bad light. I never dodged from fighting anybody. If I did, I won't be where I am now." Tell it to the less-informed, his critics assert.

And what is sure for now is that Pacquiao does not have originality in his articulations, even in his confessions. No boot camp with a styled retraction program would allow him to engage in an about-face without saying, "Punishment has been complied with thank you, Sir!" If he insists in continuing with what he's doing, he continues to cheapen the importance of his presence in congressional sessions and hearings. Pacquiao must now know that Arum's prescription entails more side effects than therapeutic implications into his total personality. Avoiding a Mayweather fight might just keep Top Rank's image intact than if it takes a devastating tool on its marketing game to watch a badly beaten Pacquiao in the hands of Arum's most hated enemies in the market today.

But for Arum, it's always his own protocol that prevails. It's just like that, at least to dramatically wait for the best time and season to beat Mayweather, Jr., better yet in his old age, all to lessen the harsh effects of Pacquiao's declining glory. And, for Pacquiao, it's safer to jump high at Arum's command. Call it "passing the buck," but if Pacquiao so wants to face Floyd Mayweather, Jr. next, he can surely overpower Arum's proposition regardless of differential standing they both have relative to the possible negotiations that must take place. Arum's job is to promote or market Pacquiao's choice, not the other way around.

Should Pacquiao just wait for Mayweather, Jr. to turn 36 with the remote possibility of making the fight happen? What's lighting up is that the power of choice ultimately belongs to Pacquiao. Now that Mayweather, Jr. issues challenges, the vindication of the judgment would be upon Pacquiao, less to Arum. Playing with rhetorical statements such as "I want Mayweather next" does not warrant surety. Nor would it enhance his *la memoria de cajon*, "Whoever the fans want me to fight, I will fight him. I am just a fighter; it's up to my promoter," would give the fans truism.

Pacquiao sings the same old song, "My Way," and once again plays double-faced cards taught by his partners in poker games. Oh, yeah, no more memory-based statements; the paying boxing public wants it soon. The world is not getting any younger. And the ninety-four-year-old boxing fan along the streets of Los Angeles wants it soon. Yes, sooner than 80-year old Arum wants.

Is Pacquiao just trying to cover up his declining popularity? With Pacquiao's generosity and high spending power, he can summon for his own cause a whole class of brilliant writers and media institutions to drumbeat his public image above error and irresponsibility, however debunkable his intentions are.

What the boxing fans want to see is the manifestation of what is being said. That's what the paying boxing public in the American soil wants to see. Now that Pacquiao has become both a showbiz man and a political figure, if we add up all the family drama he's engulfed with and all other controversies, can the boxing fans still regard his words as trustworthy, if not meritorious? Or, is he just playing with his fans' minds and the media?

Mayweather, Jr. is probably the least of all options at this time. In fact, many a key figure in Team Pacquiao has reservations if Pacquiao is still bent on wanting the Mayweather fight at this stage of his career. It may be well to remember that-Juan Manuel Marquez, whom Mayweather, Jr. gave no round of victory in their twelve rounds of boxing and whom Pacquiao had fought twice prior to their trilogy, sent Pacquiao to boxing clinic last November. It's like the same trend is creeping into an apocalyptic mess on Pacquiao's image, both in boxing and politics.

It's pathetic but true. Pacquiao's fight fans dissipate and so does his political ascendancy at the national level in the Philippines. His dream of becoming president of the Philippines has become a flickering forlorn hope. Sure, millions of dollars would be there even before his fight night with Mayweather, Jr., if it happens. But, the post-traumatic pain and distress might be so overwhelming and devastating.

One thing is sure, Pacquiao will no longer be facing a dehydrated, electrolyte-imbalanced champion nor will he be facing a muscle-wasted Miguel Cotto or Oscar de la Hoya. He will be facing every ounce of Mayweather, Jr.'s power-cells and springing muscle mass at the full scale of a welterweight.

No longer will he be facing a disoriented fighter who would just stand in front of him, in that he can just take punches and move in and out and does his circling moves without fear of getting knocked out. Pacquiao will face the most agile and the true grandmaster boxer of this era.

If Pacquiao so faithfully intends to fight Mayweather, Jr., I would so reverently respect his case. Conversely, I am still optimistic that the Pacquiao-Mayweather fight is going to happen. Whether it is soon or before the close of 2012 or sometime in the early spring of 2013, Pacquiao must face the finest boxing scientist of this early 21st century. Nothing less, the pressure is on!

Considering its surpassing guaranteed multi-million dollars revenue potential over the record-breaking De La Hoya-Mayweather fight, it's tempting, most especially for Pacquiao's cohorts, to punctuate a date soon. And who truly cares for Pacquiao anyway? No one but Arum, who has been so protective of him.

Circus on Non-secrecy Intent of Arum's High Case-Profiling with Mayweather, Jr. – All Manipulative Disengagements?

Arum, a *Cum Laude* graduate from Harvard Law School and the current driving force behind the sport of boxing, turned eighty last December 8, and remains optimistic that "the more-than-thrice-failed Pacquiao-Mayweather negotiation would absolutely have a much better turn out this time around once it is resumed and goes final."

In an interview status pre-fight of Cotto-Margarito at the Madison Square Garden in New York, Arum says he has not yet decided which among the potential investors he would consider to be included as the prime movers of the purported Manny Pacquiao versus Floyd Mayweather, Jr. boxing event. "We have not resumed the Pacquiao-Mayweather negotiation yet, though I believe Pacquiao-Mayweather fight will happen because," for the potentially biggest fight of the century, "it would be very, very stupid for it not to happen," says Arum in another related interview with Examiner.com. Like Arum, Mayweather, Jr. also disclosed early this week saying, "I am waiting. There's no negotiation with Pacquiao camp yet at this time."

Reports in recent weeks have it that Michael Koncz, embattled and so-called less-powered adviser of Pacquiao, visited Mayweather, Jr. in Las Vegas. But, "it may have been that Team Pacquiao was simply trying to reach out to Mayweather, Jr. and talk about the potential fight, which is normally a pre-negotiation stage and nothing more," that which Arum has confirmed. And therefore, no negotiation exists between the two camps, as of this date of publication. As usual, Koncz has no clear word of the "alleged" resumption of the Pacquiao-Mayweather negotiation. "No specific details," in fact, "are yet being presented to Floyd Mayweather, Jr. And, clearly, there's no negotiation taking place yet at this time," notes one popular member of Team Pacquiao who spoke on condition of anonymity.

"If my friends from Team Pacquiao say that the Pacquiao-Mayweather negotiation is almost a done-deal, they are just fooling (Manny) Pacquiao. They must understand the legal process. Talking about it among themselves with anybody or somebody even if such person is a party to the contract does not mean to say the negotiation has started. They are all ignorant of the legal process and that includes some of the writers. Please highlight that word 'ignorant' in your article. I don't mean to insult. I am just telling about the true status. When Mayweather, Jr. says that 'no negotiation is yet started at this time', he is right," he adds.

Meanwhile, Arum, believing the fight itself will generate tremendous sums of money, says: "I believe each fighter can possibly make more than 50 million US dollars from their fight. We will find in the weeks ahead when the negotiation starts."

Arum, who is in the process of prospecting, however, declines to disclose the specific names of the investors. He believes making their names public relative to this Pacquiao-Mayweather negotiation would be a betrayal of trust and confidentiality. But he says, "The investors would be mainly US-based, some of them with partners outside of American soil." He continues, "Definitely, the fight would be staged in the US. We will announce the relevant details in due time once we formally meet Floyd Mayweather, Jr. and his party."

I still believe Pacquiao versus Mayweather, Jr. is much less probable than Pacquiao versus Marquez this coming fall of 2012. Even then, the ball right now should be in Pacquiao's court. Mayweather, Jr. would rather press on a fight; he's turning thirty-six on February 24, 2013. In fact, he rather wants to fight Pacquiao in the fall and so does Pacquiao but only with hesitancy and manipulative intent with his armies of newsmen. Pacquiao, who turns 33 on December 17, should know he can't beat Mayweather, Jr. And whether Pacquiao is truthfully bent on fighting Mayweather, Jr., no one knows. There is too much drama and numerous pretensions in the Pacquiao camp. Pacquiao himself has all the sensible excuses at this time, probably foremost of which is his continued prolonged intermittent incognito at the 15th Congress of the Philippines due to his training preparations for his last four fights after being elected to Congress in May 2010. Then there's his attempt to resolve family issues before the value-added cameras and gullible journalists and still another is his redemptive efforts to correct his declining popularity through preaching the Scripture despite his becoming impotent of true humility.

He also has an unrelenting adulterated intent to prostitute the Catholic Church of his drive to win electoral votes in the high days to come, at least all to his self-glorification. Nonetheless, I still believe there's no way Pacquiao could win over the Grandmaster from Grand Rapids, Michigan. Yes, the Pacquiao-Mayweather, Jr. fight is what we've been waiting for so long after all the frustrations during the more than three failed attempts to end both camps' negotiations with a perfection of contract. Both camps would still fail. And I still believe a fight with Mayweather, Jr. is the riskiest venture for Pacquiao at this stage all because of his political ambition. He could still make big money by fighting a less threatening opponent and Top Rank's marketing game and image would still remain enhanced.

And a fourth encounter of Pacquiao against Marquez is surely less threatening now than a Mayweather fight considering the degeneration of Marquez's physiologic functions as he nears forty. I am sure Pacquiao should now be able to figure out the aging Marquez. Pacquiao should come to his own senses. He is still faster and more powerful, only with less accuracy against effective counterpunchers and only with less than surpassing technique and rhythm than the Marquez of yesteryears. But, Marquez, on the other hand, would surely feel the tool of reaching the midlife crisis of self-reservation, least that he would be much slower six months from now and onward. Just like Mayweather, Jr., on the other hand, Arum, is a marketing genius. He knows that if a Pacquiao-Mayweather fight happens this fall, a rematch of Pacquiao against Juan Manuel Marquez would die down. And it's a big loss of opportunity. Both Pacquiao and Arum have said repeatedly to this writer the Mayweather fight is not within their radar's reach. And now that Pacquiao's pound-for-pound ranking continues to be shaky and has dropped in fact closely to No. 3 all because of Pacquiao's less convincing win over Marquez in recent months, Pacquiao's cohorts would be much more apprehensive, except those who care less about his likely fall.

Marquez lost to Mayweather, Jr. via unanimous decision. And it was a shut-out victory. And that was two years ago versus Pacquiao's recent take on Marquez. Yes, "styles make fights." But Pacquiao's style as exposed by Marquez is something Mayweather, Jr. can outdate convincingly, if not just by knockout. Yes, I would not discount such a possibility of a knockout by the American icon.

While the controversy of the supremacy of Pacquiao over Mayweather, Jr. and Marquez continues to hover around in the minds of the boxing public, Arum might as well take the hot iron strike on the brightest December fireworks in Las Vegas or in Texas, nay, in Mexico, for sake of Pacquiao's security from the hands of the Mexican mafia. Pacquiao being distraught about his recent loss to Bradley may have become lukewarm to Arum's bait. But, Arum may have just studied the intelligence and saw credible evidence that there's no way Pacquiao could beat Mayweather. For him a Mayweather fight might just be a suicide for Pacquiao, affecting both his promotional and political outfits. The only success the boxing world has at this time is the science of making everyone itching to intensify the hype of such a potential fight. Yes, the pressure upon Pacquiao and Mayweather does not abate, however. Still, these two pound-for-pound boxers will have to make an unequivocal statement to brush back allegations of avoiding the fight. That remains to be seen.

PACQUIAO AT THE DEVIL'S GOLF COURSE WITH MAYWEATHER, JR.

NOVEMBER 20, 2011 – The wilderness certainly conjures up far better memories than the boxing world. But, I'll always cherish those great times I had by the ringside covering boxing's big events in this early 21st century more than what the wilderness simply offers to my sub-consciousness. And I vouch that very soon more intriguing images from the ring of madness would be showing forth their brilliance in far better energy equilibrium.

Just a few months ago, I attended a weekend camp along with the Pathfinders Club in Death Valley here in California, about 300 miles away from Los Angeles. Surviving the freezing temperature that turned our water in the dishpan into crystal formations and not cursing, for sure, I walked on the lowest point of the United States surface 282 feet below sea level at the Badwater Park by the Devil's Golf Course. Both Badwater and Devil's Golf Course, also a large span of salt, share half of the salt-bed in the said area, but Badwater is the more prominent between the two. From where I stood, holding a ten-pound salt rock with my left hand, I remembered the lefty Pacquiao's salty yet potentially weighty item with Floyd Mayweather, Jr. for their purported negotiation.

A few weeks after his trilogy with Lightweight Champion Juan Manuel Marquez, Pacquiao told the media he's willing to take a smaller share with Mayweather, Jr. just to make their fight happen. That was in December when Mayweather, Jr.'s 90-day jail sentence was declared by Nevada Judge Melissa Saragosa to begin supposedly last January 6.

Sure, out of Mayweather, Jr.'s obscurity, Pacquiao pressure with almost zero tolerance for Mayweather, Jr.'s circumstance. Why challenge a ring-fight at such a time? Playing games?

Now, Mayweather, Jr.'s jail term was moved to begin on June 1 which allowed Mayweather the chance to fight as scheduled with HBO on May 5 at the MGM Grand Arena. Upon knowing that Pacquiao had expressed a willingness to submit to a lesser purse, Mayweather Jr. jumped in like a freeman and challenged Pacquiao. Then, Pacquiao changed his mind. Pacquiao now wants 50-50 share and wants the fight closer to June 1 (end of May) intimating Top Rank Godfather Robert Arum's rationalizations that a better venue is prepared even before Mayweather, Jr. challenges Pacquiao and that such will be ready by the end of May with far more promising live gates sales and extra millions to each fighter. Is this a case of 'splitting economics' versus 'split personality'? Why is Pacquiao trying to make it so difficult this time when he can surely overrule Arum's wishes if he is really not scared to fight Mayweather, Jr.? Is he just promoting another political propaganda to rectify his declining popularity?

As of this writing, in spite of Pacquiao's all-time low rating last month at +350 improving to + 147 versus Mayweather, Jr.'s inversely defining high last month at -500 dropping to - 185, according to Sportsbetting.com, a 50-50 share would just be a less than fair share for Mayweather, Jr. who has a stronger and broader fan-base than Pacquiao: the actual American pay-per-viewers.

Therefore, if the fight were held before the close of 2012, a bet of $ 100 for Mayweather, Jr. would only win $ 54.08 in case he wins. On the other hand, a bet of $ 100 for Pacquiao would handsomely win $ 147 granting he wins.

I missed the chance to visit the Devil's Golf Course. Many have said "Only the devil could play golf" on its surface, due to a rough texture from the large halite salt crystal formations. This, I hope, is not going to be the case with Pacquiao 'golfing' around in the boxing world at the expense of the boxing fans and the Philippine flag he uses with every fight, nay, in the name of God.

At the Devil's Golf Course, Pacquiao is invincible only until his die-hard fans realize he is not. He must have felt the freezing point when Mayweather called him out, saying "Step-up, Punk!" for a fight this May 5. But is Pacquiao now playing at the Devil's Golf Course with Mayweather, Jr.'s masterstroke on one hand and a Scripture in the other?

Interviewing Pacquiao is Jannelle So, a full-time broadcast journalist known for her work as the television host and producer of Kababayan L.A. on Channel 18. She once worked at the Asian Journal Publications during her formative years in the U.S. just when this author, having worked for 10 years, resigned in 2004 from the same broadsheet.
Exclusive photo copyright @ 2012 by PACQUIAO UNDER CROSSFIRE *for Engineer Ronnie Lu & his family*

COMPLEXITY OF PACQUIAO'S WORDS: ARE THEY ABSOLUTELY RELIABLE?

*J*ANUARY 9, 2012: HOT POTATO via HOLLYWOOD, CALIFORNIA – Call it passing the buck, but if Pacquiao so indeed wants to face Mayweather Jr. next, he can surely overpower Arum's proposition regardless of their different stands relative to the possible negotiations that must take place. Arum's job is to promote or market Pacquiao's choice, not the other way around. Should Pacquiao just wait for Mayweather, Jr. to turn 36 with the remote possibility of making the fight happen?

What's lighting up is that the power of choice ultimately belongs to Pacquiao. Now that Mayweather, Jr. issues challenges, the vindication of the judgment would be upon Pacquiao, less to Arum, in fact. Playing with rhetorical statement such as "I want Mayweather next" does not warrant surety. Nor his *la memoria de cajon*, "Whoever the fans want me to fight, I will fight him. I am just a fighter; it's up to my promoter," would give the fans truism.

Pacquiao sings the same old song, "My Way", and once again plays double-faced cards taught by his partners in poker games. Oh yeah, no more memory-based statements, the paying boxing public wants it soon. The world is not getting any younger. And the ninety-four-year-old boxing fan along the street of Los Angeles wants it soon. Yes, sooner than 80-year-old Arum wants it. Is Pacquiao just trying to cover up for his declining popularity?

With Pacquiao's generosity and high spending power, he can summon for his own cause a whole class of brilliant writers and media institutions to drumbeat his public image, however debunkable his intentions are, above error and irresponsibility. What boxing fans want to see is the manifestation of what is being said. That's what the paying boxing public in the American soil wants to see.

Now that Pacquiao has become both a showbiz man and a political figure, adding up all the family drama he's engulfing with and all other controversies, can the boxing fans still regard his words as trustworthy, if not meritorious? Or, is he just playing with his fans' minds and the media? Mayweather, Jr. is probably the least of all options at this time. In fact, many a key figure in Team Pacquiao has reservations about Pacquiao still wanting the Mayweather fight at this stage of his career.

Remember that Marquez, whom Mayweather, Jr. gave no round of victory in their twelve rounds of boxing and whom Pacquiao had fought twice before their trilogy, sent Pacquiao to boxing clinic last November. It's like the same trend is heading for an apocalyptic mess on Pacquiao's image both in boxing and politics.

Pathetic but true. Pacquiao's fight fans dissipate and so does his political ascendancy at the national level in the Philippines. His dream of becoming president of the Philippines has become a flickering forlorn hope. Sure, millions of dollars would be there even before his fight night with Mayweather, Jr., if it happens. But, the post-traumatic pain and distress might be so overwhelming and devastating.

One thing is sure, Pacquiao will no longer be facing a dehydrated, electrolyte-imbalanced champion nor will he be facing a muscle-wasted Miguel Cotto or de la Hoya. He will be facing every ounce of Mayweather, Jr.'s power-cells and springing muscle mass at the full scale of a welterweight.

No longer will he be facing a disoriented fighter who would just stand in front of him, where he can just take punches and move in and out and do his circling moves without fear of getting knocked out. Pacquiao will face the most agile and the truest grandmaster boxer of this era. If Pacquiao so faithfully intends to fight Mayweather, Jr., I would so reverently respect his case.

Conversely, I am still optimistic that the Pacquiao-Mayweather fight is going to happen. Whether it is soon or before the close of 2013, Pacquiao must face Mayweather, Jr. Nothing less, the pressure is on! Considering that it promises to surpass the guaranteed multi-million dollars of revenue potential over the record-breaking De La Hoya-Mayweather fight, it's tempting, most especially for Pacquiao's cohorts, to punctuate a date soon.

And who truly cares about Pacquiao anyway? No one but Arum.

PACQUIAO CAUGHT IN HEADLIGHTS

NOVEMBER 20, 2011 – Pacquiao must have sensed by now that the political landscape he faces, as of this writing, is no longer the same source of exuberance and relative Shekinah that Arum foresaw a few years back. Filipinos are increasingly becoming divided relative to his being called a "national treasure." And nothing is less treasured than his personal life versus his political and business life. His "promotional" image is less revealing than what his secrets would tell following controversy after controversy, both public and private.

But one thing is certain, of course, in that his true hardcore supporters and the others like the sycophants, the paid hacks, the gully-wow politicians and the depressed, the disillusioned and the disenchanted, would still continue to sing hallelujahs and will even try to close in on their hero from one corner to another, even with his aggressive stance against human trafficking, Pacquiao still seemingly gets tangled up.

And like a deer caught in headlights, his case in 2012 in the boxing arena would be an inescapable requisite for his ultimate journey in politics. He might just as well walk away from boxing or just pick a fight with a less threatening opponent before he hangs up his gloves for good.

This first headlight points to what Karl Marx called the "opium of society" – religion. In fact, he wrote: "Religion is the sigh of the oppressed creature, the heart of a heartless world, and the soul of soulless conditions. It is the opium of the people." And in today's Maharlikan nation, Pacquiao has become such "opium" of the less informed, the less inspired and the less cared for, with the exceptions of those *intelligentsia* and *illustrados*. And whether you like it or not, millions still are bent on giving glory to the Maharlikan hero, especially in times like this when no one has brought "honor" to the Philippine flag more impressively than Pacquiao himself. This belief prevails despite the view shared not just by hundreds of thousands or perhaps millions of Filipinos that Pacquiao lost to Marquez. Still, Pacquiao, thus far, is the only living Maharlikan who may have bridged the social gap between the rich and the poor through his inspirational feat in the ring of madness and more, by his kindness to the less fortunate.

New clues for Pacquiao's likely choice of future opponent came from his recent controversial win by majority decision over Marquez. Arum, Pacquiao's promoter, wants the Filipino Superstar to take Marquez after Timothy Bradley. But Freddie Roach, who trains Pacquiao, prefers that his pupil face a fresh opponent. He believes a Pacquiao fight against Marquez the fourth time is less appealing.

Another equally elucidating headlight to note, Roach, who confessed that Pacquiao really did not clearly win over Marquez, now wants to abandon the idea of a fourth encounter with Marquez for Pacquiao. He'd rather have Pacquiao fight undefeated WBC Welterweight Champion Floyd Mayweather, Jr. He thinks Mayweather, Jr., being a fresh opponent for Pacquiao, poses a lesser challenge than Marquez. Conversely, it looks like Pacquiao is facing difficult odds. He already had tremendous difficulty with his last encounter with Marquez, who is a technical fighter with effective counter-punching ability. Yet, Marquez was handily defeated by Mayweather, Jr. in 2009 by winning every single round of their twelve rounds of boxing.

Now, both Roach and Pacquiao are verbally asserting a better alternative for a November fight against Mayweather, Jr. But, can this be a "bluff" knowing that a purported Mayweather-Pacquiao fight has already been getting so remote? Mayweather, Jr. wants to stay in his best comfort zone at 154 pounds of Super Welterweight while Pacquiao wants to strike at 147 pounds and below. Would this be just a ploy to pave the way for Pacquiao to pick easy fights?

Only three opponents are formidable for Pacquiao for now: Marquez, Mayweather, Jr., and Brandon Rios. Forget about Sergio Martinez. Pacquiao was just bluffing when he told the world that he is willing to fight Martinez at 150 pounds. And, that was before his third encounter with Marquez. In the past few months, on the other hand, an inside report from Team Pacquiao rather suggested to this writer that Mayweather, Jr. is not really listed as part of Pacquiao's opponents before he retires.

What more can Pacquiao defend against Mayweather, Jr., a more effective counter-puncher and a better attacker, when Marquez, the "lesser light", had exposed him to the fullest? In fact, Marquez has humbled Roach by his eventual confession, saying, "I have underestimated Marquez." And such a well-pronounced underestimation by Roach might just await Pacquiao's ultimate fall at the hands of Mayweather, Jr.

Consider this: Just before the Pacquiao vs. Marquez III, Pacquiao vs. Mayweather betting odds with the presumption that if the bout were to happen in 2012 and that if Pacquiao would win impressively over Marquez, the principle of standard deviation on a straight wager took an inversely proportional dive yet not too deep at stake: Mayweather - 145 over Pacquiao's +115. This meant that if you bet $1,000 for Mayweather on a straight wager, you would win $ 689.06. But, if you bet $ 1,000 for Pacquiao on a straight wager, you would win $1150. Hmm...it's not anymore that close after Pacquiao's less convincing win over Marquez.

Pacquiao takes a downward slope to an all-time low of + 220 versus a towering climb by Mayweather, Jr. to -300. Betting $1000 for Mayweather would only win $333.33. Betting $1000 for Pacquiao would win $2220. Now, the ball is on Pacquiao's court. Mayweather, Jr. comes forward to boxing fans and aficionados shifting the burden of approval to Pacquiao's camp. He has "reserved," so to speak, May 5 for him and Pacquiao to face off.

Like Rocky Marciano who retired in 1955 with a record of 49-0, including six successful title defenses, Mayweather, Jr. would want his record untarnished. Even then, the greatest individual rivalry in boxing nowadays centers on him and Pacquiao. Ongoing war of words between this son of Grand Rapids and the son of the Maharlikans should not last well beyond their retirement from boxing. The deciding moment should be on the night of May 5, 2012, if not beyond the year of the end of the world at least according to the Mayan Calendar.

Now, Mayweather, Jr. definitely chooses not to walk away from boxing as undefeated without demolishing Pacquiao who is also on the verge of cementing his legacy as the early 21st century king of boxing. Mayweather, Jr.'s record tells it all 42-0, bearing 61.9% wins by knockouts. Perhaps he's been considered as the most brilliant boxing scientist in our time.

Mayweather, Jr. will soon turn 35 on February 24. But, should he retire from boxing without exchanging leathers with Pacquiao? Hell, No! He has already mounted himself a better offense to Pacquiao. Recent pound-for-pound ranking for best boxers of the world has it on this writer's list: Mayweather, Jr. reclaims the helm and downs Pacquiao to flat note No. 2. One such attribution of such immediate change in the ranking was the less convincing performance of Pacquiao over Marquez, a common opponent of the two.

But, Mayweather has been considered as the top boxing gates producer alongside Oscar de la Hoya, the Golden Boy who definitely was instrumental in lighting up Mayweather, Jr.'s image even brighter on May 5, 2007 after their twelve rounds of boxing at the MGM Grand. Don Chargin was the main promoter of the event. Mayweather, Jr. won a controversial split decision. The gross live sales reached $18,419,200 out of 17,078 paid attendees, which still ranks No. 1 according to the Nevada Athletic Commission. The Pacquiao-De la Hoya fight in 2008 ranks third with $14,300,300 out of 14,468 paid live gate attendees. The rise of Pacquiao to the said ranking was clearly attributed to the Golden Boy's star power across the United States of America, along with Top Rank. It was the first time that Top Rank rose to top 5 highest grossing boxing events at gate. The Lennox Lewis vs. Evander Holyfield II ranks second with 17,078 paid attendance at Thomas and Mack with Don King as the main promoter, with gate sales grossing $16,860,300. All these three top producers were on Pay-per-View live.

Mayweather, Jr., nonetheless, has the upper hand. But for how long?

ARUM HAS THE PRESCRIPTION

*J*ANUARY 12, 2012 – Pacquiao can't go wrong by following celebrated Harvard lawyer and Arum's prescription. Its side effects may be toxic, and may have already been causing encephalopathy to the boxing minds. And for Arum, it's the safest order of the era for Pacquiao's complex affairs. It affects his business, showbiz and politics; however injurious it is to the latter's standing before his rallying, marching sycophants and less-informed supporters.

But the boxing public may have been too intoxicated with Pacquiao's playing games with Arum over counter-puncher Floyd Mayweather, Jr.'s fanfare. This is especially true after his non-convincing victory over Azteca's brilliant counter-puncher, Juan Manuel Marquez last Fall. You see, Arum knows Pacquiao is allergic to effective counter-punchers. That's why he has prescribed a remedial intervention based on what he believes are effective counter-measures to neutralize Mayweather's virulence. Mayweather would be under Arum's isolation protocol, at least in these days before another Fall to come. One thing, though, is that while Mayweather hovered quietly above Pacmania just before his 90-day jail time was reset to begin on June 1, Pacquiao began brandishing his clout with the Philippine media, saying he is "willing to fight Mayweather even with a smaller share, so long as the fight will happen." Judge Melissa Saragosa of Nevada, in a sweeping power-hold, granted Mayweather's appeal. This moved the starting date of his jail term to June 1, Pacquiao changed his gear, as Mayweather seized the chance for a May 5 fight, and declared valiantly via his official Twitter account: "Manny Pacquiao, I'm calling you out. Let's fight May 5th and give the world what they want to see. My jail sentence was pushed back because the date was locked in. Step up, Punk." Now, Pacquiao wanted not a smaller share, but a 50-50 split. Worse, he rejected the $ 40 million fixed offer as guaranteed purse from Mayweather.

Is Pacquiao playing games and becoming a non-trustworthy bubbling head?

Even then Pacquiao insists: "Whoever the fans want me to fight, I will face him atop the ring. I don't choose fights. It is my promoter who does, because it's his job. My job is to fight, everybody must realize that; I've said this over and over before and I'm saying this again, I want Floyd Mayweather Jr. to be my next opponent, and I haven't changed my choice despite recent developments." If Pacquiao is sincere in his articulations, then he should not be jumping high into the pit of destruction even if Arum says so. But, he even asks Arum 'how high?'

Pacquiao may have lost his ascendancy of trustworthiness, even before the national scene of Philippine politics. He has learned early on the wiles and ugliness of sliding from what could be called 'honorable.' He has done enough damage to his ever-respectable stature, even if the projected mega-fight materializes.

Still, Pacquiao continues to fool the public by stating, "Whoever says I'm ducking this fighter or that fighter, doesn't know me, or just plainly wants to put me in bad light. I never dodged from fighting anybody. If I did, I wouldn't be where I am now."

What is sure for now is that Pacquiao does not need an in-home boot camp with styled retraction program to engage in an 'about-face-cadet less honorable program,' so to speak. Pacquiao must know that Arum's prescription entails more side effects than therapeutic implications into his total personality. But, for Arum, it's always his own 'protocol' that overrides. It's just like that, at least for Pacquiao's declining glory. And, for Pacquiao, it's safer to jump high after Arum's command.

NO KNOCKDOWN, ONLY INCREASING DOUBTS: PACQUIAO RETAINS HIS WBO WELTERWEIGHT TITLE

NOVEMBER 12, 2011: RINGSIDE REPORT FROM MGM GRAND ARENA, LAS VEGAS, NEVADA – Renowned conditioning coach Alex Ariza rather saw a prescribed picture on fight night of November 12 at the MGM Grand Arena in Las Vegas highlighting pound-for-pound king Pacquiao versus his longtime nemesis, Marquez.

The author interviewing renowned conditioning coach Alex Ariza during the Pacquiao-Marquez 3 Press Conference in 2011 at the Beverly Hills Hotel in Beverly Hills, California.
Exclusive Copyright@2012 by PACQUIAO UNDER CROSSFIRE
for Manny Pena

"I could see Pacquiao setting out boiling moments before knocking Marquez out anytime in the first three rounds," smiled Ariza as he was heading to Palazzo Apartments after the usual treacherous outdoor training with the congressman of the Philippines. "Marquez may not see it coming."

Yes, Ariza insisted that an early knockout was likely as Pacquiao was seen giving an extra push on his training, extending extra miles to his usual regimen this time. "He is going to be too much for Marquez to bear on their trilogy," Ariza added. "He (Marquez) will freeze once he feels the impact." Ariza was referring to a single knockout punch which he believed Pacquiao would fire upon Marquez at the heat of their heavy exchanges in the first three rounds.

But, that was not the case at all. No knockdown, only doubts. And it's in the heads of the majority: the biggest robbery transpired tonight! Pacquiao retained his World Boxing Organization Welterweight Championship belt against challenger and longtime nemesis, Juan Manuel Marquez, in their twelve rounds of boxing before the 16,368 in attendance, mostly Mexicans, on a roller-coaster kind of frenzy.

Marquez, who clearly demonstrated insurmountable power and dominant techniques in their twelve rounds of boxing, failed to satisfy his supremacy over Pacquiao in the hearts of the three judges. The three judges scored the bout, to wit: Robert Hoyle, 114-114; Dave Moretti, 115-113; and Glenn Trowbridge, 116-112. Pacquiao won by majority decision.

Official final punch statistics showed that Pacquiao connected 30% total punches versus Marquez's 32%. Pacquiao threw 578 punches, with only 176 connected. Marquez threw 436 punches, with only 138 connected. In terms of jabs thrown, Pacquiao landed 59 out of 304 and Marquez 38 out of 182. As for power punches, Pacquiao landed 117 out of 274 (43%) and Marquez 100 out of 254 (39%). Total rounds gave per round average of landed punches for Pacquiao 14 out of 49 and Marquez 11 out of 36.

Though judging a boxing match is inherently a subjective experience, Marquez clearly showed dominance in clear punches, clean punching, effective aggressiveness, ring generalship and defense, except in rounds 3, 6, 9, 10 and 11, at least according to this writer.

Marquez clearly dominated Pacquiao in technique in their two encounters, though Pacquiao prevailed because of his heavier and better hand-speed. And, for some, the same may have happened tonight.

"I do not know what more I should do to convince the judges," said Marquez. "I know I clearly won the fight. . .I feel good about my performance. I made Pacquiao look really bad. He knows he lost the fight," Marquez added. Marquez said he is not sure if he will fight again. "I will have to sit down with my family and talk about it," Marquez asserted.

Arum, who promoted Pacquiao under Top Rank, believed Pacquiao-Marquez trilogy may have not helped resolve doubts at all. "This sure didn't resolve issue of supremacy between the two fighters. In fact, there were many rounds which can go either way," said Arum. "The judges would usually favor the effective aggressor especially when the fight is close."

Arum, however, said he will sit down with Marquez and Pacquiao to work out a match sometime in May. "I would have to be friendly to Mexicans, to make it happen," Arum exhorted. He intimated Cinco de Mayo as a good date. Cinco de Mayo is a Mexican Independence Day.

For Freddie Roach, who trained Pacquiao, "the fight was very close. . .But, we squeezed it out. The judges scored the fight and they have the best seats in the house. That's how they scored the fight."

"I know Marquez did well in the fight," said Pacquiao, who arrived two hours late for the post-fight press conference with a bandage on his upper orbital-superficial skin, and only spoke briefly to the media. "I know the expectation of the people did not happen," said Pacquiao. "He always backed off and always waiting for my action. I know it's not easy to fight Marquez."

"I understand we have to accept the (results) of the fight. But, just watch the fight again in the replay. I know I clearly won the fight," Pacquiao added. Pacquiao was whisked out of MGM Grand to Mandalay Bay for a dinner with his team, friends and family. As a matter of routine, Pacquiao will host tonight a post-fight party at the Mandalay Bay where he stays in which his band will highlight the celebration. Tickets are sold at $59.

Marquez fought Pacquiao in a controversial bout that was scored a draw in 2004 and in 2008 a split decision to Pacquiao's favor, all because Marquez suffered a knockdown in the third round that proved to be the difference, as the remaining rounds were scored dead even.

PACQUIAO VS. MARQUEZ 4 STIRS UP OLD ANXIETIES, PENALOSA AS RELIEVER AND GAP-FILLER

JANUARY 3, 2012 – Would Pacquiao choose to abandon a tangled thread? Untangling the same thread does not really fit Pacquiao's ability to take things with a grain of salt. That's not his strongest appeal in boxing, not even his take over Juan Manuel Marquez, the great counter-puncher. Pacquiao himself knows less about making stitches-net, maybe nothing at all.

But, he sure knows that the best fighting-cocks are those which are nearing their retiring age (between 4-5 years old) and are, depending on their innate ability, great counter-punchers and have been trained to dance on top of tangled threads, so to speak, granting they are from fearless bloodlines, such as Kelso and Hatch.

Other than 90-day jail termer pound-for-pound and pay-per-view king Mayweather, Jr., only old Marquez, Miguel Cotto and Brandon Rios are the probable three being mentioned by Arum as front-runners for Pacquiao's next fight after Bradley. But, among these three, Marquez, while nearing his retirement, still stands firm as the better draw in terms of Pay-per-View, prompting the general paying boxing public's interest to prevail.

While the opposing forces of Team Pacquiao are enjoying Mayweather, Jr.'s moratorium within Arum's frame of thought, Marquez remains the logical opponent for Pacquiao before he bumps into a much harder, clever son of Grand Rapids, Michigan. No one heeded

Mayweather, Jr.'s call. So, the ball is rolling on Pacquiao's carpet. Arum wants Marquez again for Pacquiao. Likewise, Marquez wants it but only with a condition that their fourth encounter should be held in Texas. And why not?

Let me get this straight: I'd rather sit up in my favorite US Airways for four hours with my family, with one stop in Denver, Colorado, to that seemingly quiet, lonesome Fort Worth International Airport in Dallas, Texas and check-in at the world famous Gaylord Texan Hotel for a high rate and witness by ringside the first-rate Pacquiao vs. Marquez at the Dallas Cowboys Stadium than just witnessing the same fight staged in Las Vegas at less cost plus controversies.

I don't mean to imply that having the same held in Texas would be free from possible controversies. Controversies could spring up and thrive anywhere. That's the cost of subjective human experience. Yes, it is costly for a California resident to travel that far, to Texas. But, witnessing the fight between Pacquiao and Marquez the fourth time in a neutral site would be worth the expectation a boxing fan could get.

In the world's gambling capital, Pacquiao himself, status-post fight, tried to keep posturing like one of thoughtful repose – his mood benign but rather troubled just as when he was rocked by Marquez, convincingly in their trilogy. Las Vegas surely won that fight night big time. Sports-betting centers said only about 2% at minimal dollars of the bettors for Pacquiao-Marquez trilogy went on a straight wager for a decision win for Pacquiao. The same centers said it would be a great pleasure for them to take part of the interplay of Pacquiao-Marquez episode in the fourth encounter. They said controversial fights help them keep their business going.

In a lighter vein, enterprising promoter Sampson Leckowicz told this writer in an exclusive interview that he thinks the Pacquiao-Marquez trilogy was such a close fight. Leckowicz, who was one of the key figures in making possible Pacquiao land his first US debut in 2001, said "Yes, it was a close fight but it was too far for Pacquiao to be the winner of the fight."

Even Freddie Roach, trainer of Pacquiao, reluctantly spoke out his thoughts immediately after the trilogy, saying: "I really did not know who won the fight." Like Leckowicz, Roach agreed: "It was a close fight. . .But, I don't think Pacquiao convincingly won the fight," he added.

Arum said: "It certainly was not a decisive win by Pacquiao." In fact, it created a divide between Pacquiao fans and Filipino writers. About 95% of the Filipino writers who covered the same fight by ringside, except those paid sycophants by Team Pacquiao, arrived at the same conclusion that Marquez should have won the fight at least by majority, if not by unanimous, decision.

Some key members of Team Pacquiao as well, until now, still believe Pacquiao was not the clear winner of that fight. In fact, "we would have no question if the judges, indeed, gave the decision to Marquez," one top confidant of Team Pacquiao spoke on condition of anonymity.

"We thought the best decision Manny (Pacquiao) could have gotten after the fight was a draw. Even though I am thankful that Manny (Pacquiao) got the majority decision, I still think he did not deserve it. Anyway, I won $2,150. So, what more should I complain about? Like my friends, I am just being honest with my opinion. I want him to fight Marquez a fourth time. Hopefully, he'll knock him out or win decisively and I'll win again, hopefully convincingly with bigger dollars. Marquez is turning 39, anyway. He should be slower." He continued: "We're kind of nervous about Marquez. We know Manny (Pacquiao) has been uncomfortable about fighting Marquez. But, no matter what happens, it's going to be a difficult fight for him."

At this time, a potential bout of Pacquiao against Marquez started to stir up anxiety among members of Team Pacquiao, who wanted a fresh opponent. Roach himself, who went non-traditionally to the "Marquez Science School of Boxing" for seven years, would rather avoid a fourth encounter for Pacquiao against Marquez. Roach knows nothing about disrupting the rhythm of a counter-puncher. "I rather propose former bantamweight champion Gerry Penalosa would be a great gap-filler for Roach's ineptness in some areas," he added. Perhaps Penalosa, the greatest counter-puncher the Philippines has ever produced, can help Pacquiao at last, out-smart the bravest heart of the Aztecs.

For both Pacquiao and Roach, it's going to be a humbling experience. Consider this: Pacquiao was perhaps the loneliest figure from round 4 through 12 when he fought the brave-heart son of the Aztecs, Juan Manuel Marquez, in their trilogy at the MGM Grand Arena in Las Vegas, Nevada on November 12, 2011, at least a year shy of the end of the Mayan Calendar.

"That's true: Manny Pacquiao did it all by himself after round three," said one of the key figures (number 1) of Team Pacquiao, who consented to be interviewed on condition of anonymity. "He was dealing with a trainer who may have less coherence in his thinking."

"When would you know that Roach is in the state of senility, being a victim of Parkinson's disease?" He points out that Pacquiao's trainer, Freddie Roach, is known to have Parkinson's disease, like what this author's aunt has. He is a brilliant thinker in his own right. But his brilliance, his rare determination and courage, as observed by boxing critics, are not enough to fight off the disease. This writer believes the same ailment does not have the final word. Roach knows best. Still, several in Pacquiao's circle have been apprehensive.

"That's why Manny (Pacquiao) has become a bit confused, too, and was doing it all by himself in solving Marquez's puzzle after round three because I think Freddie (Roach) himself even had no idea on how to deal with Marquez," said another key figure (number 2) of Team Pacquiao, who also consented to be interviewed on condition of anonymity.

"I wonder if Roach's Parkinson's disease and the medication he takes have something to do with his lapses during brainstorming moments," added he who claimed he had watched many closed-door sessions of Pacquiao's training and had observed Roach's tremendous decline in critical thinking – with periods of forgetfulness.

He continued: "It's obvious he's being affected by the infirmity of Parkinson's disease. You see him, you see the symptoms. His health is fast-declining. And it's affecting Manny (Pacquiao) who relies on his analysis."

According to the National Institute of Neurological Disorders and Stroke, "Parkinson's disease is a degenerative disorder of the central nervous system in which, in later stages, cognitive and behavioral problems may arise, with dementia commonly occurring in the advanced stages of the disease." "It's going to be the most difficult decision for Manny (Pacquiao)," said the third source from Team Pacquiao noting further, "Roach should now retire from Pacquiao's corner."

"If that's the case, Roach should not be training Manny (Pacquiao) anymore," he asserted thinking, "it's too dangerous for any boxer to rely on someone who is no longer the same during periods when the medications he's taking are low in therapeutic range or it could be that Roach may have been unknowingly suffering from unknown side effects. . .I have observed on many occasions that Roach is not thinking right and, sometimes, he's very hot tempered."

"I believe it's really Manny (Pacquiao) who made Roach become a great trainer, not the other way around. Not even about the chemistry of Manny (Pacquiao) and Roach. I also think Roach's health is deteriorating pretty fast and his critical thinking skills are no longer the same. It's always Manny (Pacquiao) who's finally trying to solve the puzzle inside the ring."

"Roach even confessed after the fight that he had no idea on how to intercept Marquez's fighting style. And forget about the hand speed and lateral movements that Manny (Pacquiao) has. What's bad is that Roach has really not developed something new to defeat Marquez. He's just lucky Manny (Pacquiao) is naturally gifted of power and speed and an extremely hardworking fighter."

Nonetheless, he said: "Pacquiao has the speed, power and natural intelligence but these are not enough. Roach, being a trainer, has to tap these raw materials and make something better out of them; that's needed to overwhelm Marquez's effective counter-punching ability. Roach has not really developed technically sound target plans A, B and C over the years to defeat Marquez. Manny (Pacquiao) has become so predictable with good counter-punchers."

Now, who is really to blame? Can we really blame Pacquiao for his failure to give a clear break on his last fight with Marquez despite his earnestness in trying his best in that ring of madness?

"Roach spent seven years at Marquez's science school of boxing and still not able to solve the puzzle?" Pacquiao first fought Marquez in 2004. The board of judges scored the bout as a draw. A rematch in 2008 ended with a controversial split decision in favor of Pacquiao. And then followed their trilogy last November 12 where Pacquiao won a controversial majority decision.

If Pacquiao's era were written on the Aztecs' diary in consonance with the Mayan calendar, its demise may have been so prematurely imminent even before the end of 2012. The Mayans of ancient days predicted the end of the world in 2012. And for Pacquiao, he had just entered the beginning of the period of his final crisis. And, "this, essentially in part, is all about whether or not Pacquiao needs a new trainer for his last few fights in the ring," he decries. "But we must give him (Roach) the honor for all his hard work and dedication to Manny's (Pacquiao) boxing career."

Considering Roach's attributed lapses of critical thinking, I still believe Roach is the most brilliant and hardworking boxing trainer of all time. He has given all his utmost mental energies and physiologic stimulations and inspirations to Pacquiao. Perhaps, he's the only American who can truly break the hardest of hearts among Pacquiao's fans throughout the world when he passes away. He will always be remembered. Oh yes, he will be one of reflections in my solitude and meditations. I salute the man.

HATTON MAY FREEZE THIS SPRING

Note: Author's prediction dramatically was fulfilled as published by Philboxing.com on March 14, 2009, 40 days before the fight

Regardless of who respected who, fans and pundits can expect fireworks this May 2. Rightly so, they wanted to see droplets of blood from one face or a knock out by another. And they wanted to see fighters truly fighting, not dancing. After all, it's about evolving versatility versus unforgiving aggression. But I vouched that International Boxing Federation (IBF) World Champion Ricky Hatton's unforgiving aggression may manifest an intensity of fighting only against his own fear: the imminence of getting knocked out again.

Mayweather, Jr. seen as faster, more skilled, and far more of an accurate puncher dominated Hatton, and knocked him out in the 10th round to retain the welterweight championship on the cold night of December 8, 2007 before the wild sold-out crowd of 16,459 at the MGM Grand Garden Arena in Las Vegas. Most of the fans in wild cheering mode had come all the way from England to support their hero, the then-undefeated "Hitman" of 43 professional fights. Striking his best at 140 pounds, Hatton had his worst.

Pacquiao surely got the better of Hatton's first loss, if not just capturing Mayweather, Jr.'s blueprint. Pacquiao would have to gobble up yet another opponent in a sensational performance. Hatton would simply be outgunned, though he would never stop trying to win a round or two. But it would surely be entertaining and convincing to watch as Pacquiao enhanced his historic resume by claiming his sixth title in six divisions.

I had a brief conversation at the Wild Card Gym with Igor Frank, a friend of mine who regularly writes for *Burbank Times*. Pacman was in his training session. Igor told me that Pacman would just be too good for Hatton.

Michael Moorer, the new training assistant of Freddie Roach, also had this to say: "Pacman is too fast, too agile, and too powerful for Hatton." Moorer's boxing record of 52-4-1 speaks volumes of his ring savvy as he faces Pacman during mitts sessions. A southpaw himself boasting 6'2" with an imposing 245 pounds, Moorer takes charge of training Pacquiao at Wild Card while Roach is out preparing Amir Khan, former sparring partner of Pacquiao, for his fight today against Marco Antonio Barrera in Lancashire, United Kingdom.

Banking on his signature right uppercuts and lightning lefts, Pacquiao may have transformed himself again from being a foreseeable aggressor into an evasive, effective counter-puncher – a precursor to his gaming rooster-like frontal attacks. Sure, it will be a fast-paced, exciting fight with a momentum that may somehow shift back and forth but not to be outdone, Pacman will press forward. He will consistently outwork Hatton. At least, that's what I have issue-spotted during his warm-up shadow boxing sessions at the Wild Card Gym in Hollywood.

And there will be more surprises. Remember, Pacman has just gained more mileage from his spectacular win over Oscar de la Hoya. Always expect the unexpected as Pacman surges to another level. Nevertheless, Hatton must keep his defense tight because once Pacman unloads his neurovascular-surgical shots in succession of five to seven, Hatton may just freeze this late spring.

Two great fighters hailing from two empires strike back from the ends of the earth: one for supremacy, the other for redemption, staging "The Battle of the East and West" on May 2 at the MGM Grand Arena in Las Vegas, Nevada.

MARCH 30, 2009: ROOSEVELT HOTEL, HOLLYWOOD, CALIFORNIA – Beckoning us back to the glory days of Old Hollywood, two great men crossed paths today at the Roosevelt Hotel but joined in a symmetry of sportsmanship over indignation – all for supremacy versus redemption, in fact.

Hatton, an international superstar hailing from Manchester, England, said: "I will give Manny Pacquiao a hell of a fight! I am the stronger and the bigger man!" Pacquiao, officially proclaimed a National Treasure by the Philippine government, said: "I respect Hatton because he is a nice guy. But, in the ring, we will fight for freedom."

Two great boxers – one from England, the other from the Philippines, both modern heroes in boxing, and in the realm of influence outside the ring of violence, bringing the spotlight back to the historic Roosevelt Hotel that stands as the cornerstone of the Hollywood renaissance, where luminaries hosted their first-ever Academy Awards ceremony in the Blossom Room in the early 1900's.

Pacquiao (48-3-2, 36 KOs) and Hatton (45-1, 32 KOs) scored their only pre-fight press conference in the United States hot and raw, garnering tremendous response from the mainstream media, banking on the potential of a great fight for the International Boxing Federation Light Welterweight Championship this May 2 at the MGM Grand Arena in Las Vegas, Nevada.

Hatton, *Ring Magazine* 2005 Fighter of the Year, will defend his title. But, he will enter the ring as the underdog against the undisputed current Pound-for-Pound King of boxing, Pacquiao. "It's going to be the fight of the decade," said Richard Schaefer, chief executive officer of Golden Boy Promotions. "We have two great fighters who are willing to give their lives in the ring," he added. Asked about how he compares this promotion to others such as the Oscar de la Hoya vs. Floyd Mayweather, Jr. fight, Schaefer said: "Well, the De la Hoya-Mayweather Event was a big fight. But we have Ricky Hatton who fought last year in front of over 58,000 people in England. And we have Manny Pacquiao who is arguably bigger than the President of the Philippines! So these two are clearly the most popular fighters in the world today. They deserve the red carpet right here on Hollywood Boulevard." Asked further as to how he sees the fight: "I think strength and size would matter most." He said, "Ricky Hatton has the edge, considering that he is undefeated at

Hatton May Freeze This Spring

140 pounds, and he has fought great fighters including Luis Castillo of Mexico, and Kostya Tszyu of Australia." But, Top Rank Godfather Bob Arum firmly believes that Manny Pacquiao has the speed and power much greater than what Ricky Hatton can deliver.

Meanwhile, Floyd Mayweather, Sr., trainer of Hatton, disclosed his game plan for dethroning the Pound-for-Pound Champion of the world. "The game plan is to rock Pacman to the rope, and to take him down twice with body shots," he said in comical flair. "Hatton will not only take him down; he will take him out." Mayweather, Sr. bragged himself as the "smartest trainer having the smartest fighter."

"So how the hell can you lose?" He further predicted that "Hatton will knock him out in five rounds." Freddie Roach, however, said he believes otherwise, saying, "Pacquiao will take him [Hatton] out in three rounds."

Hatton confessed that his main problem is Pacquiao's speed. But, he said he believes he has better footwork than Pacquiao, and that it would be much easier for him to outbox the latter.

Pacquiao, whose faith in God and his boxing career are somewhat inseparable, maintained his usual response saying, "Nobody knows who will win on May 2nd." In a rhetorical fashion, he added, "Only God knows." Pacquiao further declared: "We just have to pray that nobody will get hurt, including the undercards." He said he considers this fight as the toughest one of his boxing career. Elated and upbeat, Pacquiao told the VIPs and the media that he is looking forward to play cards with Hatton after the fight, that they will be friends afterwards.

Meanwhile, what had become a great night at Roosevelt was not without tremendous support from fans that flooded across Hollywood Boulevard, and rushed toward the stage fronting the news media, and eventually entering forcibly into the lobby of the hotel. Many celebrities attended the event as well. Among them were Hollywood Actor Mark Wahlberg who, before he started acting, was best known as Marky Mark – the pants-dropping rapper who attained fame and notoriety with his group the Funky Bunch, and another American football star, McGuinness. Because of the excellent marketing mix by the promoters, and the support the event gets from a wide range of audience, the anticipation is growing and the 20 x 20 foot canvas set on stage at the MGM Grand Arena in Las Vegas will soon be painted into a black and blue masterpiece the world is anxious to see.

UK'S MOST FORMIDABLE SPORTSWRITER PREDICTS PACMAN BY TKO

The author with Gareth A. Davies, boxing correspondent from The Telegraph Media Group, and Robert Jorgensen, publicist of Sky Sports, in London.
Photo taken on April 4, 2009 inside the Thai Restaurant near Wild Card Gym in Hollywood, California.
Exclusive Copyright@2012 by PACQUIAO UNDER CROSSFIRE.

*A*PRIL 4, 2009: HOLLYWOOD, CALIFORNIA — It's an all-time high here with HBO and other news media crews, with Team Pacquiao and teams of sparring partners enduring the 72 degree Fahrenheit heat at the Wild Card Gym paradoxically warmer than ever, as Pacquiao, after the vigorous afternoon training sessions, readies himself to tackle a two-hour exercise with his left hand fine motor skills to sign-on boxing gloves, T-shirts, and photographs that boxing fans from different walks of life present to him.

What fortifies the afternoon frenzy is the presence of two journalists from London: Gareth A. Davies, the formidable sportswriter from the *Telegraph Media Group*, and Robert Jorgensen, publicist of *Sky Sports*, the Rupert Murdoch-owned satellite TV broadcaster who will facilitate the telecast of Hatton vs. Pacquiao on pay-per-view in the United Kingdom.

Davies and Jorgensen just arrived from London, prompting to conduct round-about interviews with the training camps of the legendary Maharlikan hero Manny Pacquiao and of Ricky Hatton, currently in Las Vegas, Nevada entering the last quarter of his training with self-proclaimed best trainer, Floyd Mayweather, Sr.

Davies and this *Maharlikan Times* writer, along with boxing commentator Leoncio Royo, Jr., exchange views and pre-fight analysis about the Pacquiao-Hatton event on May 2 at the MGM Grand Arena in Las Vegas, Nevada. Beholden to neither boxing camp, Gareth A. Davies brings along with him his invisible crystal ball from the United Kingdom. It reveals to him nothing short of mere speculations. But he sees from it a see-saw fight between Pound-for-Pound King Manny Pacquiao and IBO Light Welterweight Champion Ricky Hatton but conversely predicting an inevitable full stoppage in the 8th or 9th round.

Asked about how he sees the fight other than his prediction of a late stoppage by Pacquiao, Davies says, "Hatton may dominate Pacquiao in the first three rounds." But "Pacquiao will catch up with Hatton through the fourth to fifth rounds and will clinically land more punches until the eighth or ninth round." Hatton, whose only caveat is whether or not he is more powerful and heavier than the Filipino phenom, "may not get the better of Pacquiao's super-speed and incredible lateral movements - super crablike - striking from different directions naturally which will call situations that he may not be able to hit Pacquiao effectively, and may become less effective with his aggressions," Davies adds. Nevertheless, Davies does not discount Hatton's great ability to super-impose his power to brawl, and his fighting spirit to withstand Pacquiao's likely vicious attacks. "A perfect punch to the body just as what he did to Jose Luis Castillo of Mexico in their WBC International Light Welterweight Championship/IBO Light Welterweight Championship in 2007 which ended by TKO in fourth round may not be a remote possibility," Davies warns.

BRIEF PROSE FROM BLUE'S CLUES FOR HATTON: DON'T PLAY 'LUCKY 9' WITH PACQUIAO

MAY 1, 2009: LAS VEGAS, NEVADA - British Knight Hatton may not be puffing a smoking pipe. But he has plenty of fire that may have boldness to nullify the odds-makers who put him below par. Hatton says: "Forget about the odds-makers' qualifying numbers. I am going to shock the world."

No doubt, Hatton's confidence rather surges to a higher level. His only loss to Mayweather, Jr. at 147 pounds may serve him as his lesson-book and springboard for his fight against Pacquiao. He has drawn such confidence from being the undefeated one at 140 pounds. His great knockout performance over Paul Malignaggi in the 11th round on Nov. 22, 2008 may have some clues as to how much improvement he has made since his memorable fight with Kotstya Tszyu in 2005. Pacquiao and his trainer, Freddie Roach, have studied his fights very well.

Yes, Hatton has shown vulnerabilities. He cannot contain heavy body shots. In fact, Tszyu almost got him down with one. HBO's 24/7 Episodes have shown that Hatton still lacks lateral movements and rhythm to employ effective boxing skills. And with this, his brain by far cannot just develop a critical pathway that fast in a span of a few months of training. Hatton may have neurovascular paralyzing shots, but they won't just come along with fine lateral movements. Pacquiao is too quick to catch him in the eye, and too agile to shun his treacherous trail. For one thing, neuromuscular therapy takes years to fortify its desired outcome, except for the versatile or gifted one. Hatton's basic instinct will surely dictate his own pace once he gets hurt badly. And forget about what Mayweather, Sr. has taught Hatton. His pupil is likely to waddle in the dirt.

Rightly so, Hatton may not be able to waltz with Pacquiao, in as much as he tried to do with Malignaggi, who is much slower and less powerful than the former. Nevertheless, Hatton may need to set up a trap for the Pound-for-Pound King to draw his card closer, in that they would have to engage in close combat. That's the only chance he could possibly hurt Pacquiao with a "perfect shot" on the body, just as what he did to Jose Luis Castillo in 2007 which ended TKO in fourth. And only if he is lucky enough. That's the only way he could impose his size and power at close range, at least according to his calculation. And Hatton knows that.

Meanwhile, as for his trainer, Floyd Mayweather, Sr., his poetic intervention truly pleases everyone. Style, speed, sixth sense, and synergy of power – Pacquiao has them all, and is bound to make Hatton fall! And here's the final clue from Blue for Hatton: Don't play "Lucky 9" with Pacquiao, for he will surely fight you with pure boxing skills.

A MOMENT OF PREDICTION, A MOMENT OF REFLECTION

*M*AY 2, 2009: LAS VEGAS, NEVADA – It's 2 o' clock in the morning and soon enough, Hatton will reassert his supremacy at 140 pounds against *Ring Magazine* Champion and Pound-for-Pound King Pacquiao, for the former's IBO Light Welterweight Championship belt in the forefront of the world stage at this luxurious MGM Grand Garden Arena.

While each spectator anticipates to join the roaring crowd at the beginning of the night, this date, and just a few hours from now, and to try to inspire with madness and chanting for their respective favored fighter just when that illusive time comes, Pacquiao and Hatton rather have found their respective solitude for better composure, if not contemplation.

As these two great men prepare for the "Battle of the East and West" and cool off their minds, boxing prophets are still delving into heated debates, if not exchanging friendly notes of predictions, at the hottest boxing forums and corners of the earth. And it seems like the pundits and fans have crossed their paths, and have exhausted all arguments as of this writing. The momentum has shifted to some sort of "wait-and-see" introspection.

Nevertheless, nobody has really given a clear-cut reading of the crystal ball. Even this writer would surely fail to give a near-perfect clue despite his boldness in many instances. Forget about predictions for now. It's amazing to note what many see from both fighters this moment. It is an intriguing aura from each of these humble icons. It is the sense of serenity that they both embrace before they will enter into that potentially-stormy 20 x 20 foot canvas set on stage which has been painted in a black and blue masterpiece that the world is anxious to see.

The anticipation of this fight is probably a record-breaking one that may surpass the Mayweather-Hatton fight, and possibly the Pacquiao-De la Hoya fight as well, all because of the prospect of excellent marketing mix by the promoters, and the support this event gets from the wide range of audience across the continents, nonetheless. In fact, tickets for the boxing arena are sold out. And tickets for closed-circuit viewing are close to sold-out too, according to the Top Rank officials. The Pay-Per-View sales volume is likely to yield a record high.

Despite the fact that I am rooting for Pacquiao, I am not discounting the possibility of an upset. Hatton does have plenty of fire to nullify the odds-makers. He has tasted the bitterness of his first defeat at the hands of Floyd Mayweather, Jr. on December 8, 2007 at the 147-pound division. Such defeat rather has been his lesson-book and springboard of motivation as a matter of avoidance of pain. Hatton is a pragmatic optimist in his own right. And he is motivated more than ever, probably more than Pacquiao's content.

Hatton's lone mission: To default the tectonic shift in boxing that the Pacman has bolted across the Pacific to this land of milk and honey, and to the European continents in the process. Now it's our turn to enter into the apparent twilight zone – a moment of prediction, a dawn of reflection – in fact. But will the Pacman Era be cut-short?

BLOODLESS BUT BRUTAL AS PACMAN STOPS HATTON IN ROUND 2

MAY 2, 2009: LAS VEGAS, NEVADA – Onto the canvas, he fell down like a helpless tree, as if struck by a lightning bolt – unconscious, in fact, before he landed straight on his back – flat with his eyes rolling back up. Then, both of his arms involuntarily unfolded to his side, then motionless, in fact, as Referee Kenny Bayless knelt by his side assessing his countenance for about ten seconds, as if forgetting to count. Then, Bayless raised his own right hand waving, signaling a full stoppage of the fight that took place at 2 minutes and 59 seconds into round 2. That was the fallen brave heart of England, Hatton, now the former IBO Junior Welterweight Champion. And that was probably the breaking moment that Pacquiao left his opponent behind unmindful of his unconscious foe – vindicated perhaps.

What prompted that scene may have been Hatton's willful fastening of Pacquiao's right forearm while punching the latter to the kidney and upstairs on several occasions. Pacquiao became fired-up toward Hatton, hammering with his right hook that dropped the latter kneeling with his own elbows to the forefront, as if bowing for prayer in the first round.

Hatton got up to beat the count and then, as the fight resumed, another barrage of punches came through heavily from Pacquiao's right hand. At this time, Hatton fell to the canvas again, on his back toward his corner. Quickly, he regained his composure, and delivered brief exchanges with the Filipino superstar five seconds before the bell rang to end round 1.

Round 2 opened up with Hatton assaulting Pacquiao with good jabs and a quick shot to the head. That slightly stunned the latter. Pacquiao took hold of the brief exchanges, tactically avoiding Hatton's game plan to wrestle him again, firing lots of right hooks upstairs – some missed – and then that gruesome lightning left bolted to Hatton's right jaw punctuated the end of the fight, and the raucous crowd of 16,262 at the MGM Grand Arena and millions more watching all over the world momentarily shifted their haste in a catatonic state – shocked at what they saw – while the Hatton family had their eyes fixed toward their own hero stretching flat in the middle of the 20 x 20 foot canvas that the world had been anxious to see.

And the chanting in the melody of "Winter Wonderland" by the Britons that began, "There is only one Ricky Hatton," vanished in thin air. Then new lyrics of the same music reverberated across the arena: "There is only one Manny Pacquiao."

"That was astonishing!" said my seatmate, one of the sportswriters from the UK. "I am amazed at Pacquiao's speed and power – unbelievable!"

Freddie Roach said:" I had watched hours of film of Hatton - I knew him better than my own fighter. Hatton pumps his fists before he throws. . .Hatton was wide open for the right hooks. I knew Pacquiao will take him down within three rounds."

Pacquiao landed 73 of the 127 punches against Ricky Hatton in just 5 minutes and 59 seconds, including 34 of the power punches in the second round. Hatton connected on only 18 of 78.

Pacquiao captured the IBO Lightweight Welterweight Championship belt and was still the *Ring Magazine* Junior Welterweight title holder. His record improved to 49 wins, 3 losses, 2 draws and 37 knockouts, while Hatton dropped to 45 wins, 2 losses and 32 knockouts.

CONTRASTING SIGNS: IDEALIST VS REALIST HARKING IN THE WORLD OF PACMANIA

*J*UNE 23, 2009: THE LAND OF PROMISE; MINDANAO, PHILIPPINES – There's never a minute of forgetting how much Pacquiao – "the Philippines' National Treasure" – lost his bid for the congressional elections in the first district of South Cotabato four years ago. It was an event wherein the incumbent Congresswoman Darlene Custodio scored a swift, knock-out victory.

Of course, the images of victory by Custodio have not faded in the mind of Pacquiao. But, the deployments of some words of encouragement from his close associates keep coming – convincing him in fact to run again for Congress in another district, specifically in Saranggani where the Chiongbians reigned for decades.

And so I must say this forthcoming match-up would be a great topic that can fire up a hearty discussion. Meanwhile, let me share with you my perspective and tenacious attempt to get back into the trail of politics, charging on the mind of an idealist versus a realist.

I grew up in a family where tidbits of political news had exceeded its share far more substantially than the frequency of my daily meals. It was all pathetic at times. Talks about both local and national candidates on countless occasions broke the meal etiquette to the consummation of our table topics. One such topic was about the political ideologies relative to political candidates and to those in power. I will never forget the thrill of delving into the circumstantial bliss of the politicians' respective ascendancy.

And even during my college years, I carried the same influence to entertain my fervor. Activist by heart, I fought my way to the march-rally at Silliman University in the late 1980's. Being one of these busybodies in campus, I did my own inquiry with the League of Filipino Students as to the issues these political candidates and incumbents were facing.

That was during the leadership of Judito Cabusao, the long-time president of the League of Filipino Students and Editor-in-Chief of the Weekly Sillimanian, and by the way, Cabusao was definitely not a personal friend of mine. But he unarguably had a great mind, especially in any lengthy, hot-air debates which I usually delved into during our Philosophy studies at Silliman University in Dumaguete City, Philippines, more than two decades ago. His heart had lived enough by faith and his bearing by intellectual foresight and must have transcended the national boundaries. In fact, he was once a major proponent for the independence of East Timor and in the expose of rampant abuses in the early 1990's, both civil and political, striking their contrasts from the domestic to the international scene. He was not just an uncompromising risk-taker and a fearless grassroots activist but a great thinker as well. At least that was my best recollection of him and it's something one must ponder upon. Nevertheless, indifference of ideological impressions was what truly separated us.

But I thought he was an ideal man to become one of the great public figures of the Republic of the Philippines – a man who still deserves my respect, at least in the realm of political idealism. And I must say, nonetheless, he had the strength of a modern "tao" (man) that remains potent in the heart of a true Maharlikan idealist.

And as for this day, we have a paradigm shift. It's a case worth studying for this generation and onward. It's not about mass demonstrations and burning effigies. It's about giving reverence to that remonstrance regarding them as far more deserving in the legitimacy of our democratic appeals. Yes, political mass rallies may have just become the unbreakable mirrors of the past. And one such "mirror" convicts the image of the past. But, through it all, one can look into the long vista of hope for a phenomenal version of a revolution.

But the modern thinking of "tao" actuates his analysis with much introspection versus retrospection. That's the very fabric of a revolutionary man – a visionary man, in fact!

Yes, we have the lens through which we can see clearly the imminent new political dispensation and we pray that it may heal the injuries by simply capitalizing the grief of the Maharlikan nation. And regardless of political enchantments, Filipinos by far thrive in the best exclusion of oneself on the will of assertiveness especially in the area of politics.

Meantime, we search from the tip of the Philippine archipelago way up to the other end from one generation to another. Still, we have just engulfed our idealistic findings as something illusory, in our quest to find another enabling realist who has the ability to capture the pulse of time. A pragmatic one in his own right, "Emmanuel Pacquiao, a Congressional seat aspirant in the Alabel district of Sarangani, Philippines, is just the right man for that position," according to Gina Dayao whose parents still live in Sarangani. And, even then, "now is the time for him to revolutionize politics especially in the national level. We need a sensitive, and a naturally intelligent man to keep the vision of Mindanao alive," she added.

But, unlike Mr. Cabusao, for purposes of illustration, whose intelligence unquestionably renders Pacquiao void of academic honor, one may need to scratch deeper into his own scalp to study and to learn the intellectual gem of being a Congressman. "It's not just about implementing projects in his designated district," said Marlene Flores, who claimed to have many relatives in Sarangani. "It's about knowing himself into the standing of being a lawmaker."

"It's better for him to run for Governor or Mayor," said Roy Torres who hails from General Santos City. "He has no idea about the job of a congressman, nor does he have the skill and education to tackle such position, if ever he gets elected." But, "he may win in Sarangani, if ever he runs for Congress and he may be able to improve the lives of the people in his district."

However, Torres further supposed that Pacquiao's intent to narrow the gap between the rich and poor in the matter of addressing the needs of that purported district as for a congressional seat and as to his sincere desire to emerge into the intricacy of legislative role rather breaks the traditional propensities of a common politician, at least to his own intimation.

"Pacquiao may have just shown enough novelties to become the "Deliverer" that he wants to be, far better than any of the incumbents in the Philippine archipelago, transcending, in fact, the walls of the political academe," Torres added. "One thing I am sure, the public eye may be less harsh to Pacquiao than an ordinary entrant to politics," said a former professor of Mindanao State University who consented to be interviewed by this writer on condition of anonymity. "His credible achievements before politics bring the tide of acceptance in the hearts of the general populace of Sarangani. He may have less resistance in there than what he once had when he fought against Darlene Magnolia Antonino-Custodio."

Nonetheless, Pacquiao is determined to undercut the pressure of misgivings inherent of politics, banking on his own ideological values and moral ascendancy necessary to promote the well-being of the lone district of Sarangani.

But what about those numbskull politicians, scoundrels and the sycophants, whose adulterated intent might bring the tide of eventual destruction to the world of Pacmania? When shall their egocentric machinations abate? Will there be a repeat of the fiasco when he ran for the first district of South Cotabato? Of course, no one can divine. But the signs will not stand out until Pacquiao spells out the world of Pacmania. To this end, I render my respect. But unless Pacquiao embarks on a stronger machinery, engaging his political affairs free of influence from these traditional politicians and " jolly-golly-wows", his intent to epitomize the fulfillment of his dream for the Land of Promise =Sarangani - may just remain a flickering forlorn hope, if not an idealistic reverie.

COTTO ADVISED BY FELLOW PUERTO RICAN TO WEAR EYE-PATCH

SEPTEMBER 16, 2009: BEVERLY HILLS, CALIFORNIA – Despite suspicion that Antonio Margarito may have used the same illegal wraps on his hands during his fight just before his loss to Shane Mosley and led to the revocation of his boxing license for at least one year by the California State Athletic Commission, the story of the Puerto Rican's devastating defeat at the hands of the former can no longer be reconstructed.

But forget about his first professional loss. Cotto's situation as to his fight against Pacquiao this November 14 at the MGM Grand Arena in Las Vegas, Nevada, runs perilous to a much more embarrassing defeat of the Puerto Rican, according to Pacquiao's close associate, who disclosed game plans to this writer on condition of anonymity.

"Pacquiao's hammering fists are more fatal upon impact than that of Margarito's illegal wraps," he added. Conversely, "Pacquiao's speed, power and agility are obviously far superior than the WBO Welterweight titlist," said Freddie Roach, Pacquiao's celebrated trainer, when asked by this writer yesterday during the Media Press Conference at the Beverly Hills Hotel in Beverly Hills, California. He, however, conceded that, "It's going to be a difficult fight."

Asked again by this writer about his game plans if ever Cotto employs dirty tactics during the fight, Roach said: "We have prepared some counter-strategies for them and we are ready. . .We have studied his fights and we see he has some troubles fighting a southpaw," Pacquiao, who is a southpaw himself, said as he sat by the table surrounded by media interviewers.

Wearing a Herringbone black-tweed cap and in his fine-touched, black suite, Pacquiao seemed to be at his best composure, usual winsome spirit and remained not apprehensive about Cotto's record, size and strength.

Cotto's record of 34 wins and 1 loss shows his impressive victories over all of his three opponents in recent years who are southpaws, namely: Zab Judah in 2007 by TKO 11, Carlos Quintana in 2006 by RTD 5 and De Marcus Corley in 2005 by TKO 5. On the other hand, Pacquiao's tactical skills still seem unpredictable because of his powerful right hand that bolts almost equally of his tectonic left as seen in his last two fights against Oscar de la Hoya and Ricky Hatton. As for Cotto, he said he is "ready to win over another great southpaw" and "ready to give a clean fight."

"I have no excuses and I am training much harder for this fight," said Cotto. "I am ready to go back to Puerto Rico after the fight as a champion and bring home another belt."

Cotto was referring to the new WBC Diamond Belt which was created as an honorary championship belt exclusively for fights between elite boxers. The belt is handcrafted by an artisan in Mexico City (Chilango) with 18 carat gold fusion and has about 800 diamonds, emeralds and rubies, as well as 150 Swarovsky semi-precious stones, which this writer has touched, examined and had photographs of himself as well with it – holding it close to his chest, in fact.

"Manny Pacquiao, a three-time WBC world champion in three different weight divisions, and Miguel Cotto, a former WBC International champion, are unquestionably qualified as two of the best boxers of today," said Mauricio Sulaiman of the World Boxing Council.

One writer asked Cotto of his tendency to get cut and bleed easily above his left eye as seen in his fight against Joshua Clotty, which can quickly change the tempo of the fighting style.

Cotto said: "Well, I have to be ready for it." Meanwhile, there is still one chance of escape. "Cotto has to wear a black eye-patch alternatively during his training." At least, that's the tactical input of Tony Vasquez, a Puerto Rican bearing 6'1" and a veteran boxing strategist in his own right, who worked his way up as a fighter and retired from the United States Marine Corps.

Vasquez, a boxing tactician who claimed he is not associated with the team of Cotto, shared some concerns about Cotto fighting against Pacquiao. On the other hand, Vasquez, who happened to engage in a conversation with this writer right after the media conference, would love to share his wisdom to Cotto or to any boxer on how to become an effective fighter against Pacquiao.

"To be effective," he said, "Cotto must prepare for the worst scenario wherein he will have to fight with one eye open unless the fight is stopped by the referee or ring doctor, or by his team." He added, "Pacquiao's almost equally powerful bilateral fists, his speed and the complexity of his footwork must be the major problem of Cotto."

"Using a black eye-patch on one eye during his sparing sessions will help him widen his peripheral vision, explore new dimensions and gain better control of his range if it happens that one of his eyes is swollen-shut," Vasquez further explained intimating that his techniques may have not been used yet by boxing trainers, as of this writing.

"Despite what will happen when that time comes that he would only have to rely on one eye, the skills that Cotto has learned will become his contingent tools for victory, and that he must not give up," added the 68 year old son of Puerto Rico who claimed to have lived by the beautiful mountain ranges, notably the Cordillera Central, which rises to 4,389 ft (1,388 m) in the Cerro de Punta.

LESS UNDERSTOOD NEURO-SCIENCE OF BOXING: THE JET-WEIGHT THEORY OF CONSERVATION

SEPTEMBER 24, 2009 – I will never forget the thrill of witnessing a boxer at the emergency room whose admitting electrolytes in the blood were as follows: Potassium 2.2 (3.5 to 5.5 millimeter-equivalents per liter), Sodium 112 (135 to 145 millimeter-equivalents per liter) and "the miracle mineral," Magnesium 1.1 (1.7 to 2.2 milligram per deciliter). According to report, this athlete 5'7" weighed 154 pounds on the tip of the scale during the official weighing, weighed 181 pounds when he was admitted at the hospital. He was over-hydrated and malnourished.

Then, in less than two hours, another boxer was admitted who looked drained and malnourished as well, 5'10" in broad body frame but weighed only 147 pounds on fight night, of which his usual pre-fight weight was 154 pounds But, as for this fighter, he tipped off the scale at 144 pounds after three months of some sort of "body-conditioning", they said. He was impractically tamed to live in the third world country where the scarcity of food made its mark as headlines in the newsprint, which de la Hoya somehow was put to a poignant test.

Well, Frank Lotierzo of *Sweet Science* must have said it well and unknowingly must have helped me expound my talking points when his article got published on September 22, 2009, and my article as well, "Jet-weight is Mayweather, Jr.'s story of a boxing scientist," surfaced on the newsprints on September 21, 2009. Lotierzo's article was titled: "Cotto should emulate Mayweather, Jr. and weigh-in at 147."

Now, let's talk about the Mayweather, Jr. and Marquez weight issue and my theory. "Jet-weight theory of conservation," as coined by this writer, is void of newness at all. But, as to the world of new trend in boxing, it is one of direct attempt of subjugating the very intent of "catch-weight." In fact, it corrupts or forfeits the very purpose of catch-weight acclamation.

As of this writing, I received 2038 e-mails commenting on my article published last Monday regarding "Jet-weight" is Mayweather, Jr.'s story of a boxing scientist. Of these numbers, I spent nearly six hours spot-reading their respective contents. To my surprise, the majority gave good comments. But, I would like to address one out of dissenting thirteen who clearly misunderstood my supposition. And for the senders, I thank you for expressing your opinions.

Here's one of the comments: "Your moronic comment doesn't appear to be convincing to me. If Floyd is not foolish, he shouldn't agree to fight at the agreed weight of 144 pounds. He has no honor then! That's why lots of people call him Fraud Mayweather. He should fight the real welterweight then!" My take: The fight as per the agreed change in the contract was at catch-weight of 144 pounds binding in the Welterweight limit of 140 to 147. In other words, Floyd Mayweather, Jr. had the latitude of freedom to deviate from the agreed catch weight limit of 144 pounds on the condition that he pay the penalty as stipulated or adhere to it so long as "he tries to work it out" on such time of official weigh-in, which he did. But he weighed-in at 146 pounds – still a pound below the Welterweight limit of 147. And as reported, the contract was agreed to by Marquez as manifested by his signature, to work it out within the Welterweight limit.

However, both parties also agreed that any excess of weight on the official weigh-in carries a penalty of $300,000 for each pound. And the contract and its inclusive terms remained enforceable to materialize the fight, as clearly discussed and as they made sure no one exceeded 147 pounds on such exact time of official weigh-in, where Mayweather made it to 146 lbs.

Therefore, there's nothing wrong with Mayweather's tactical plan, if, indeed, he ever planned to deviate from catch-weight. That's his choice. He paid the price for his choice, which he deemed as his best alternative course of action. Likewise, there's nothing wrong with Marquez's choice of just reaching 142 pounds during the weigh-in.

But what truly set their choices apart was a matter of principle and understanding of their own philosophy along with the pulse of time, in that the fight must transpire considering the millions of dollars being spent for the campaign: "Number One versus Numero Uno."

And here's the complexity of their respective choices: it's operative and can only be rescinded unilaterally at the option of Marquez. Marquez did not pursue this option, believing that he could still weaken and take down Mayweather, so he agreed to all terms and simply penalized Mayweather by having him pay $300,000 per pound of the excess based on the agreed catch-weight limit. Otherwise, there could have been no fight at all last Saturday unless another counter-offer was agreed upon.

Conversely, in any event, this was something foreseeable. So, why sour-grape when the "grape juice" has turned into "unfermented wine"? That's part of sweet science! My proposition about "jet-weight theory of conservation" has become an effective, winning ploy only for those who understand the effective management of fluids and electrolytes in their body. I think Mayweather understood its significance and the trap of "catch-weight."

It's nothing new at all. Size does not translate to strength and speed but in Mayweather's case, it successfully enhanced both, if not physiologically maintained his metabolic advantage.

Meanwhile, whatever my supposition in that said article as commented should not be treated as mere intellectualization but a rhetorical one. And it can be "moronic" as one said, or I must say it is "viagratic" by intimation. That's the intricacy of my theory potentially rationalizing a tactical counter-strategy for low riders of "catch-weight."

And let me tell you this: If only de la Hoya opted to this supposition, he could have "pulled his trigger" and nullified Freddie Roach's nagging statement that "Oscar de la Hoya can no longer pull the trigger." What if De la Hoya weighed-in at 147 pounds at such time of official weighing and entered the ring at least 10 pounds or a bit more and not necessarily becoming over-hydrated? What if Oscar de la Hoya's transport of oxygen through his hemoglobin was one of a healthy athlete? What about his muscles which, in some way of his momentary stupor in the ring, had been so poor in tone and mass, if not edging into the state of becoming lethargic? And, what about his thinking process being affected by all these imbalances? When Pacquiao fought De la Hoya, was it just about the speed and style of the former that made the big difference? Was it just about the display of the law of physics? Or, was it not also about the invincibility of the law of physiologic balance? Yes, it's all about the balance of fluids and electrolytes as well. And I call it: "The Jet-weight theory of Conservation."

THE GOLDEN REMATCH: PACQUIAO VS. DE LA HOYA

APRIL 21, 2010: LOS ANGELES, CALIFORNIA – Getting a straight smile can be puzzling, especially from the multi-millionaire philanthropist, de la Hoya. Such transpired when De la Hoya hosted a ribbon-cutting ceremony officially marking the grand opening of his namesake high school, the Oscar de la Hoya Amino Charter Junior High School, in Boyle Heights in Los Angeles on October 29, 2009. Asked if he still has the heart of a fighter and contemplates of surprising "one-comeback" in the ring to fight Pacquiao, De la Hoya only responded to my query with an unwavering smile. And the same penetrating smile had lingered when he graced another event at the White Memorial Hospital in Los Angeles that day, when he was asked the same question.

De la Hoya is the major donor of the major building renovation of White Memorial Hospital, a Seventh-Day Adventist missionary institution founded by Ellen G. White, where his mother, Cecilia Gonzalez-De La Hoya, was hospitalized and died of breast cancer in 1990 at the age of 38. She had always hoped that her son would win a gold medal at the Olympics and her untimely death gave De La Hoya a concrete goal for the golden years onward.

When two of boxing's biggest attractions, this Olympic gold medalist and 10-time world champion "The Golden Boy" Oscar de la Hoya and current Fighter of the Decade Manny "Pacman" Pacquiao collided in a catch-weight welterweight showdown on

December 6, 2008, boxing fans invoked its reality as the type of epic match-up that fight fans dream about as "The Dream Match."

It was such a day of infamy for De la Hoya who was defeated – one-sided – via TKO in the eighth by Pacquiao but relatively not under the mercy of a physiologic observer who understands the interplay of fluids and electrolytes in a catch-weight boxing match. Consider reviewing the article I wrote early last year: "Less understood neuroscience of boxing: The Jet-weight Theory of Conservation."

I will never forget the thrill of witnessing a boxer at the emergency room whose admitting electrolytes in the blood were as follows: Potassium 2.2 (3.5 to 5.5 millie-equivalents per liter), Sodium 112 (135 to 145 millie-equivalents per liter) and "the miracle mineral," Magnesium 1.1 (1.7 to 2.2 milligram per deciliter).

According to reports, this said athlete, 5'7" weighed 154 pounds on the tip of the scale during the official weighing, weighed 181 pounds when he was admitted at the hospital. Sure, he was overhydrated and malnourished.

Then, in less than two hours, another boxer was admitted who looked drained and malnourished as well, 5'10" in broad body frame but weighed only 147 pounds on fight night, where his usual pre-fight weight was 154 pounds.

But, as for this fighter, he tipped the scale at 144 pounds after three months of some sort of "body-conditioning," they said. He was impractically tamed to live in a third world country where the scarcity of food made its mark as headlines in the newsprint, which Oscar de la Hoya somehow was put to test.

Meanwhile, Frank Lotierzo of *Sweet Science* must have said it well and unknowingly must have helped me expound my talking points when his article got published on September 22, 2009, and my article as well, "Jet-weight is Mayweather's story of a boxing scientist," came out in the newspapers of September 21, 2009. Lotierzo's article was titled: "Cotto should emulate Mayweather and weigh-in at 147."

Now, let's talk about the Mayweather and Marquez weight issue and my theory. "Jet-weight theory of conservation," coined by this writer, is void of newness at all. But, as to the world of new trend in boxing, it is one of direct attempt of subjugating the very intent of "catch-weight". In fact, it corrupts, if not forfeits, the very purpose of catch-weight acclamation.

As of this writing, I received 2038 e-mails commenting on my article published last Monday regarding "Jet-weight is Mayweather's story of a boxing scientist." Of these numbers, I spent nearly six hours spot-reading their respective contents. To my surprise, the majority gave good comments. But, I would like to address one out of dissenting thirteen who clearly misunderstood my supposition. And for the senders, I thank you for expressing your opinions.

Here's one of the comments: "Your moronic comment doesn't appear to be convincing to me. If Floyd is not foolish, he shouldn't agree to fight at the agreed weight of 144 pounds. He has no honor then! That's why lots of people call him Fraud Mayweather. He should fight the real welterweight then!"

My take: The fight as per agreed change in the contract was at catch-weight of 144 pounds binding in the Welterweight limit of 140 to 147. In other words, Floyd Mayweather, Jr. had the latitude of freedom to deviate from the agreed catch weight limit of 144 pounds on the condition that he pay the penalty as stipulated or adhere to it so long as "he tries to work it out" on such time of official weigh-in, which he did. But he weighed-in at 146 pounds - still a pound below the Welterweight limit of 147. And as reported, the contract was agreed to by Marquez as manifested by his signature, to work it out within the Welterweight limit.

However, both parties also agreed that any excess of weight on the official weigh-in carries a penalty of $300,000 for each pound. And the contract and its inclusive terms remained enforceable to materialize the fight, as clearly discussed and as they made sure no one exceeded 147 pounds on such exact time of official weigh-in, where Mayweather made it to 146 lbs.

Therefore, there's nothing wrong with Mayweather's tactical plan, if, indeed, he ever planned to deviate from catch-weight. That's his choice. He paid the price of his choice, which he deemed as his best alternative course of action. Likewise, there's nothing wrong with Marquez's choice of just reaching 142 pounds during the weigh-in.

But what truly set their choices apart was a matter of principle and understanding of their own philosophy along with the pulse of time, in that the fight must transpire considering the millions of dollars being spent for the campaign: "Number One versus Numero Uno."

And here's the complexity of their respective choices: it's operative and can only be rescinded unilaterally at the option of Marquez. Marquez did not pursue this option, believing that he could still weaken and take down Mayweather, so he agreed to all terms and simply penalized Mayweather by having him pay $300,000 per pound of the excess based on the agreed catch-weight limit. Otherwise, there could have been no fight at all last Saturday unless another counter-offer was agreed upon.

Conversely, in any event, this was something foreseeable. So, why sour-grape when the "grape juice" has turned into "unfermented wine"? That's part of sweet science! My proposition about "jet-weight theory of conservation" has become an effective, winning ploy only for those who understand the effective management of fluids and electrolytes in their body. I think Mayweather understood its significance and the trap of "catch-weight."

It's nothing new at all. Size does not translate to strength and speed but in Mayweather's case, it successfully enhanced both, if not physiologically maintained his metabolic advantage. Meanwhile, whatever my supposition in that said article as commented should not be treated as mere intellectualization but a rhetorical one. And it can be "moronic" as one said, or I must say it is "via-gratic" by intimation. That's the intricacy of my theory potentially rationalizing a tactical counter-strategy for low riders of "catch-weight."

And let me tell you this: If only Oscar de la Hoya opted to this supposition, he could have "pulled his trigger" and nullified Freddie Roach's nagging statement that "Oscar de la Hoya can no longer pull the trigger." What if De la Hoya weighed-in at 147 pounds at such time of official weighing and entered the ring at least 10 pounds or a bit more and not necessarily becoming over-hydrated? What if Oscar de la Hoya's transport of oxygen through his hemoglobin was one of a healthy athlete? What about his muscles which, in some way of his momentary stupor in the ring, had been so poor in tone and mass, if not edging into the state of becoming lethargic? And, what about his thinking process being affected by all these imbalances? When Pacquiao fought De la Hoya, was it just about the speed and style of the former that made the big difference? Was it just about the display of the law of physics? Or, was it not also about the invincibility of the law of physiologic balance? Yes, it's all about the balance of fluids and electrolytes as well. And I call it: "The Jet-weight theory of Conservation."

PACQUIAO SIGNALING A NEW LIGHT TO PHILIPPINE CONGRESS

*F*EBRUARY 12, 2010 – Amid heated demands for him to bow out of the race, Pacquiao stays silent but broadens his base in the grassroots. His calling, for one thing, touches the hearts of the electoral voters than the incumbents. In fact, his foray into politics eloquently meets the challenge of revolution. Without heat, without despair, he lives in the vortex of the troubled present, swept by dissonances of change and radicalism, but survives with the rarity of his faith and his perception intact. That's what exactly the culture of politics that our "National Treasure" must tackle in his days of trials in politics and in the sphere of dignity, hope and vision.

Pacquiao has exemplary qualities as a leader. Even Monsignor Roger Fuentes vouches the unmatchable kindness and sincerity of a man borne out of simplicity and divine fortitude: "He is a very kind person, naturally intelligent and very religious; in fact, he defines kindness by his unconditional acts of helping the poor," says the cleric. In fact, "Pacquiao has brought healing to others who are sick and dying," says Thelma de la Cruz, a fan who hails from Sarangani. On the other hand, a seventy-six year-old Filipino immigrant who claims to have received a seventeen-pound turkey from Pacquiao says: "I could live longer than I should as long as I could see my living hero." She says she first met Pacquiao when he gave out dressed turkey to the less-fortunate and fans at Temple Park in Los Angeles just before the Thanksgiving week of 2008. She says she grew up in

Sarangani and came to the U.S. 10 years ago, upon the approval of her green card under sponsorship of her youngest daughter.

Regardless of social class disparity, Pacquiao continues to enthrall the public eye, even the high ranks and the extremists of the Philippines. Rightly so, he is the "saving grace" of the Queen, President Gloria "La Gloria" Macapagal-Arroyo, whose administration is marred by allegations of corruption and misgivings.

In the Philippines, whenever he fights, crime drops to zero. The Maoist New People's Army, armed Islamic separatists and peasants in the hinterlands pay homage to the might of the Maharlikan king as he readies himself to fight in the ring at a moments' notice. Radio sets pierce the thin air in both rural and urban areas as everyone tunes in to the live coverage translated to their native tongues.

The usually huge attendance in the Catholic masses and other Christian church services are reduce to small groups, if not their schedules are changed to an afternoon celebration to honor Pacquiao's victory. Traffic congestion in the crossroads of Metro Manila and in other major cities, such as Cebu, Dumaguete, Bacolod and Davao, drops to at least sixty percent.

And there after all, one could see the mysterious conversion of someone having a recalcitrant bent. . .singing and dancing in jubilance because the old faith of a true Maharlikan has shown to their world a new light in the dawn of hope and moment of inspiration.

Nonetheless, he is the pride and joy of the oppressed and repressed. Monsignor Fuentes must be right when he says, "Pacquiao must have the appointment of God to inspire the less inspired and uninspired and the less admired when he claims he heard a mysterious voice of God in his wakefulness at one moment during one of his early days in boxing. Once again, we will not experience the same magnitude of his might as was before but from now on in a much larger scale than ever. His mighty influence upon the lives of the Filipinos, both private and public, is beyond measure.

Truly, we need not go beyond our historical experience to judge the man's heart. His heart has brought light to both young and old in matters of gaining new perspectives about life's challenges – the perspective of not giving up despite failures and pressures from the outside. Anyone who has lost sight of the inspiration that the modern Maharlikan hero sheds to this generation and onward must have seen the crass hypocrisy of other politicians and lackeys who have become the masters of none and whose lips are laden with promise and hope. But, Pacquiao has done more than just what the Maharlikan nation expects. In fact, he has already exceeded his share of unselfish thread way more a public servant must do.

Yes, Pacquiao is the true remnant of the faithful and a catalyst for change in the lone district of Sarangani. What more could Pacquiao do when his simple endorsement to any candidate can even boost one's acceptability in the hearts and minds of the voting public? And what more could he not do to bring change and improvements to the lives of the people he wants to serve? Many of our active participants in the electoral process may not have heard the midnight cry. In fact, our distinctive message is not often heard anymore because of our likelihood to pre-judge and relegate the best of our judgments to the back burner.

Here is the present truth: Our society needs more than just legislation, and Pacquiao can certainly offer more than legislation. Pacquiao is a new light who has a new message. A new growing movement must take place which can be helped and strengthened by whatsoever the political will has to offer.

The Philippines has been in a vacuum for inspiration since the declining period of influence of Dr. Jose Rizal, whose 1896 military trial and execution made him a martyr of the Philippine Revolution. Nevertheless, Pacquiao, the modern thinking "tao" or man, sends the powerful message of faith across the archipelago that he embodies the true spirit of altruism and servant-hood. He applies the biblical stand of stewardship and self-sacrifice as he tries to close the gap between the rich and poor at his own intimation.

Soon, Pacquiao will have to be tested, and the footmen in the campaign trails and sorties will have their days anew. Even so, Pacquiao has a saving faith experience that will remain fastened to the Most High. He is the man who will go beyond the fellowship and love you find most at potlucks and picnics. He feels that he just cannot abdicate his responsibility of possessing a special gift for public service. His love for public service could bring out the best of Sarangani more than mere papers and numbers would in the Congress.

Conversely, his settling truth ranks the accolades in matters of engaging the politics of achievements. Pacquiao himself is an epitome of a new revolution in the altar of achievements. And that's what the lone district of Sarangani needs as it responds to the pulse of the times.

Pacquiao must be ready for a big change in Sarangani. Whether or not Pacquiao has the full backing of the local leaders of Sarangani, he can be assured that he has the hearts of the people whom he wants to serve. Just as in the same fashion, Jocelyn Limkaichong of the first district of Oriental Negros, has toppled the Paras dynasty that once ruled for over twenty years; even when she had no mayors, local incumbent leaders or barangay captains to add to her campaign sorties, Pacquiao will have to adopt the same strategy. He should have the beat of his feet and of his true henchmen heard in the hinterlands to win the hearts and minds of the people in much the same way the grassroots and the rest of the voting public must mobilize proactively to guard the sanctity of their conscience. "Vigilance is the key," says another immigrant who just came back to the US from his vacation in Sarangani. He says he also joined the MunaTo Festival, a celebration of the rich cultural heritage of the province with the most number of native Blaan and Tboli residents, who love Pacquiao and regard him as the "Pearl of Sarangani". MunaTo is a Blaan term for "first people".

However, the honesty of Pacquiao's leaders will be tested whether they are really for Pacquiao and for the people or just for their deep pockets in anticipation of the huge campaign fund for this 2010 national election. "Beware of those 'fake defectors' and self-serving sycophants," warned Ricky Torres who hails from the second district of South Cotabato, where Pacquiao lost his congressional bid in 2007 by a margin of about 40,000 votes to Darlene Custodio.

Torres said, "Pacquiao does not have the best political machinery, but he has the hearts of the people of Sarangani at this time." Torres just had his two-month vacation with his family in South Cotabato and also spent a month in Sarangani where he claims to have a small farm of pigs and cows. He said Pacquiao has a chance to win his congressional bid in Sarangani – at least according to his friends and relatives who are residents in the said district.

He further said Pacquiao is a hot prospect to become a good congressman and the leaders there are better and faithful than what Pacquiao had in the first district of South Cotabato. "They are more God-fearing and simple in living," he opines. "Pacquiao should keep his candidacy and I know he will win by split decision this time." This writer just hopes that when the political dusts settle in the late night of May 10, 2010, Pacquiao will come out in the tally victoriously. Consider this: A landslide victory is definitely not a remote possibility, only if he uses his financial power judiciously.

Pacquiao too elusive, if not magical, for a 'Jet-weight Cotto'

November 6, 2009: LOS ANGELES, CALIFORNIA - I witnessed how the Coyotes beat the Los Angeles Kings last night at the Staples Center in Los Angeles before the upbeat crowd of over 18,000. Coyotes' victory was less tight at 6-3. Speed and elusiveness were the differential factors of the power play. Nevertheless, it has been a tumultuous off-season for the Coyotes, who have endured bankruptcy and a recent coaching change. The franchise was put under bankruptcy protection in May and Coach Wayne Gretzky quit nine days before the start of the season.

I watched the game; I thought I can somehow impart to Cotto some wisdom from the hockey rink. Cotto can only focus on what he can control as much as what the Los Angeles Kings attempted to do. I think Pacquiao's speed and elusiveness might be too much for Cotto, unless he starts using now an eye-patch alternatively on either eye during his training sessions - which, of course, neither the Coyotes nor the Los Angeles Kings ever did - to improve his peripheral vision and to control his range and angular dimensions. That, I insist it can help him evade some whistling discharges of Pacquiao's left and right crosses.

Of course unlike the Coyotes, Cotto does not need to deal with a surface for ice-skating or roller-skating. Not even Pacquiao. But, Cotto, flat-footed that he is, has less chances of remarkably asserting his agility over Pacquiao's style of a cock-fighting Kelso. He lacks fast lateral movements. I suppose Cotto's bigger face is simply an easy moving target.

In the past two weeks, I reviewed nine tapes of Cotto's last fights. And what I can draw from all angles is that catch-weight King Pacquiao would be too elusive, if not magical, for "Jet-weight Cotto." I say "Jet-weight" in the sense that, like Jet-weight King Fraud Mickey May, Cotto is likely not to comply with the catch-weight limit and may rather pay the penalty, if there's any, simply to conserve his natural size and strength. And it's going to be far worse if Cotto tries to get to catch-weight limit as stipulated. What I see is that Cotto should now be a full Welterweight fighter, basically at 147 pounds limit, by any stretch during fight night, if not at 154 pounds for the Super Welterweight.

And never forget, Cotto is capable of showing ring generalship over Pacquiao but may not have enough overwhelming recompense for defense, that the latter would just shine through out of sweet science like a diamond in the making as he surges to another level and once he feels the intensity of heat and pressure in the frenzy air of the MGM Grand Arena of Las Vegas, Nevada, this November 14.

Meanwhile, I received 238 e-mails this weekend inquiring about my take on Cotto-Pacquiao fight. They asked me so because they said I have been a bit accurate with my predictions of all Pacquiao's fights in the U.S., inclusive of his loss to Eric Morales in their first encounter on March 19, 2005. But, hold on to your conviction. Your reliance on my suppositions might be detrimental to your betting. I am not a boxing prophet. Nor am I beholden to a crystal ball's spirit of prophecy.

Conversely, bloodless as it was told, I'd rather want you to check on my intimation on Pacquiao versus Hatton which was brought to light in my article dated March 14, 2009, "Hatton may just freeze this late spring!" and we all know that Hatton indeed froze.

Another article dated December 3, 2008, which highlighted the prospect of Pacquiao's dominating performance over De la Hoya, captured the hearts of faith: "Pacman's Mighty Fortress, Bolstering His Aura of Invincibility" was where I made a prediction that as for the Pacquiao-Cotto fight, Cotto will bleed into submission. And, it's going to be Pacquiao by brutal knockout again!

RAISING THOUGHTS OVER THE HILLS OF LAS PULGAS

*N*OVERMBER 9, 2009: HOLLYWOOD, CALIFORNIA – Boxing predictions are often said in hypocrisy, as powerful honorary prophets preach to aficionados and fans about the virtue of honesty, hard work, and other qualities that they themselves generally lack. Several predictions are cases in point. In the unwarranted malignity of internet and newsprint writers, wishful thinkers cross the path of these prophets who would rather enforce "condemnation" than "correctness" upon a fighter.

In predicting the outcome of Pacquiao vs. Cotto, dubbed "Fire Power" on November 14, 2009 at the MGM Grand Arena in Las Vegas, Nevada, one said: "Cotto will knock out Pacquiao in seven rounds." And this would surely ignite debates across the land of Pacmania, most especially in the forums where madness hits the core. But how about Pacquiao winning by knockout within five rounds?

Although I am not swayed nor dumbfounded by HBO's 24/7 for Pacquiao vs. Cotto hypes showcasing the strengths and weaknesses of both camps, I still think both episodes become less dramatic than otherwise electric. But, of course, I have my own version. I just had a short vacation recently in San Diego, California. And on my way from Los Angeles through Freeway 5 south bound just before Oceanside, I passed over the hills of Las Pulgas, of which inspirations of thoughts made my day.

It is true that "pulgas" means "koto" or "lice" in the Cebuano dialect. I never intend to inspire an anecdote of Cotto in this context. And it does not make sense at all. Even then, it does not qualify as a pre-text. But I expect an upbeat Cotto trying to impose ring generalship in the first two rounds, seeking his finest angles, firing body shots and trying to flex lots of jabs again and again, acting like a horse that had just been short-tamed or had just escaped from harm's way and found a new ring to explore.

True, just the mere fact that he gets the crack at fighting the pound-for-pound king brings a lot of excitement on his part. The challenge he unleashed against Pacquiao just before he lost his bid to Margarito in July of 2008 unexpectedly met its end with an answer of a fight this November 14. Forget about the exhibitions on HBO 24/7 that downplays Cotto's speed and power in the series of episodes we view. It's less impressive and less substantive. Cotto is better than those scripted scenes.

And take this: I vouch his jabs may throw off Pacquiao's timing especially in the first two rounds. And with Pacquiao's attempts to inflict four to five combos, Cotto is likely to mix up his uppercuts and may try to dig inside, which would somehow give Pacquiao a bit of a problem.

But Pacquiao's straight left may send Cotto fewer nerve signals in a way that he would feel it as more fatal than Margarito's illegal wraps, even in the second or third round if there's more time left. I see what I saw in Cotto versus Judah wherein Cotto had problems with Judah's straight left. But most of all, one thing is clear here: Pacquiao has better stamina than Judah. And Cotto would find this insurmountable because of Pacquiao's inherent hand speed and unpredictable footwork. But, Cotto will do anything he can to survive round 4.

If one were to see the true Cotto, then it is his fight against Ricardo Torres in 2005 that must be worth focusing on. Torres got his worth in the arms of Cotto in the first round with an initial knockdown and then Cotto got his in the mind of Torres who kept coming forward with bomb after bomb and dropped him in round 2 after taking voluminous shots to the body and upstairs. And watch Cotto's deliberate quick shot to the left thigh of Torres as he delivered a series of combos and sucked up Torres' unrelenting advances in the same round.

Then, with the intention of favorably affecting deeper inflammatory processes to Torres's right thigh and lower abdominal quadrant, Cotto successfully fired five to six low-blows in the 3rd round, right before the eyes of referee Dave Fields. Yes, Fields must have lost his mind, as if he was watching a sexual act. . .just having his eyes fixed, if not suspended at the ill-doings of Cotto in many instances. Or, he just lacked sleep from his previous night outings. In fact, Cotto held his composure and still deliberately dug another low blow, causing a knockdown in the 4th. Torres was clearly the better fighter on that night, if not the spoiling, fatigue-inducing low blows of Cotto.

Yes, it was a night adulterated by the worst referee and the dirtiest fighter ever. But, as for Pacquiao versus Cotto, Pacquiao's style of a fighting cock Kelso would make Pacquiao appear illusive, yes. . .elusive as well. Meanwhile, what took place in Cotto versus Torres should not have a repeat on fight night of November 14, 2009. Referee Kenny Bayless should render a drastic measure, if the same incidents happen. Pacquiao must press on for a knockout within five rounds.

Take another look at Cotto in his fight against Mosley. Mosley overestimated Cotto by being too cautious and waited only in late rounds. He could have knocked him out even in one of the early rounds had he started early – quick and fast – and kept throwing lefts to the head. Cotto could have bled into submission. But, instead, Mosley chose the "Old Fashion Quaker Oats Brand" style of cooking versus the "Quick Brand" than can be cooked in less than five minutes, as in the case of imposing his ring authority over his calculating foe in Cotto in the early rounds.

Rightly so as for the celebrated boxing guru's plan, as soon as the opening bell rings on fight night, "We will not give Cotto a single chance to think effectively," said Freddie Roach during an ambush interview by this writer at the Wild Card last Thursday. "We will distract his thinking process by way of Pacquiao's display of speed and ring intelligence."

At this stage, Cotto should be less concerned about countering Pacquiao's surgical attacks. That's a given. Pacquiao will engage him at close range and then disappear. But, Cotto's rising confidence may just drop once he starts to bleed. Pacquiao may give Cotto a deep surgical cut in the left eyebrow from the former's hammering right, that if he won't try to run. That I think he won't do. And it is likely to happen between the third and fifth rounds, if a knock out does not steal the high intensity of the fight. Cotto should be concerned about his bleeding tendencies. And what he needs on fight night is a fast coagulating agent. And forget about Pacquiao's style because Cotto will surely face an elusive one, if not just an elusive bomber.

INTIMATIONS AND PREDICTIONS FROM PACQUIAO CIRCLE

NOVEMBER 10, 2009 – I got a chance to mingle with some of the mighty arms of Pacmania recently at a Thai Restaurant by the Wild Card Gym in Hollywood, a place reminiscent of my memorable interviews last spring with Gareth Davies - the formidable English sportswriter from the Telegraph Media Group - and Robert Jorgensen - the publicist of Sky Sports, the Rupert Murdoch owned satellite TV broadcaster who covered the telecast of Hatton vs. Pacquiao on pay-per-view for the United Kingdom.

Well, Guillermo "Jimmy" Zuno, an enterprising boxing veteran both as a trainer and as a manager from the Philippines, predicts Pacquiao to win by way of knockout either in the 4th or 5th round. A humble supporter of Pacquiao in his own right who traveled all the way from Florida and a former special agent in the Armed forces of the Philippines, Zuño keeps a low profile but does not hesitate to be bold enough of his assessment of Cotto vs. Pacquiao believing that his prediction will come to pass.

Another boxing veteran who takes pride about the nice ring on his left middle finger that bears the name of Manny Pacquiao on bluish crafted edges, Benedicto Delgado stands firm saying that Pacquiao will knock Cotto out in the 5th. Fondly called "Manong Ben," Delgado says Pacquiao's punches are as pointed as the corner of a square. "Masiyado'ng kanto, eskuwalado," declares the former trainer of Pacquiao who made his mark when Pacquiao first fought in the U.S. against Ledwaba in 2001. He believes that his protégé has more than what he needs to take down Cotto within fifteen minutes from the opening bell.

Manong Ben confesses his sense of fulfillment being Pacquiao's confidant as well for more than a decade. He discloses Pacquiao has a ritual to observe after every fight, won or lost. "Pacquiao gives three dozens of eggs to the Augustinian Monastery in Manila every after his fight for mysterious reason." He has started giving the same ever since when Sister Superior Marcos was still alive, according to Manong Ben whose knuckles and palms are still firm and thick even at his retiring age.

Tijuana Cheat, a Feasible Pick of the Four M's Status Post "Fire Power"

After his devastating defeat at the hands of Mosley and his one year suspension to legally fight in the U.S., Margarito is looming from the dust of shame. Contrary to popular opinion, he is now likely to shake off such dust and hatch out to emerge victorious over the other three M's: Marquez, Mosley and Mayweather.

Sure, Golden Boy and Freddie Roach would not like this idea. But as a matter of responding to the pulse of the times, Margarito is the most viable, if not the most logical, choice to consider after the climax of "Fire Power." Bob Arum's belief in the theory of economic utility would dictate the choice for Pacquiao's next opponent. And forget about the malignity of the "Jet-weight Theory of Conservation." Nothing is better than just having less resistance in the negotiations, as least in matters of pitting another in-house fighter against the pound-for-pound king if a rematch of Pacquiao and Cotto becomes less foreseeable.

For one thing, Margarito's brutal victory over Cotto, though the former is under suspicion of using illegal wraps, remains black and white. That gruesome incident is still alive in the memory of boxing fans. Arum would rather stifle Golden Boy Promotion's power over its pursuit of Pacquiao for Mosley or Marquez and much more forestall a debacle on another possible match with Jet-weight King Fraud Mayweather. This is most important because at this point, Pacquiao seems to have reached the highest limit of his basal metabolic index that could keep him more effective at catch-weight in the welterweight division.

If Cotto fails to deliver a convincing performance for a rematch with Pacquiao, then Arum would surely seek his own measure in the media that pushes to drum up the name of Margarito in the eyes of the boxing public. With this in mind, boxing fans should forget all about the hype and underestimations; Top Rank Godfather must prevail. Oh, yes, Margarito is likely to be penciled for a March fight with Pacquiao. A fight between these two gladiators at 144 pounds catch-weight limit should be fair enough. Jet-weight by-passer should be onerously penalized, I suppose.

The other three M's, Mayweather, Mosley and Marquez should just spend their wishful moments for a much lesser retirement package. And of these three, the probable next is Marquez. But he must wait his turn until after the Tijuana Cheat retires once more.

Blame it on the heat. But it's all about having a less bumpy and a much easier critical pathway. And when all else fails, all competing inroads qualifiers would still depend on Arum's power of choice. After all, Pacquiao would just say: "I am a fighter and it's all up to my promoter."

Being the Top Rank Godfather of power, intelligence, love and the lord of his own thoughts, Arum holds the key to Pacquiao's selection. But wait a minute my friend, these are all just my intimations, plus wishful thinking versus predictions over the hills of Las Pulgas.

WATCH MIGUEL COTTO TONIGHT MORPHING INTO A HOPELESS "PHARAOH"

NOVEMBER 14, 2009: LAS VEGAS, NEVADA – It's 3 a.m. and the arguments are coming to a close. And as the scanty clouds begin rolling over the dazzling Las Vegas strip this chilly, misty moment, fight fans are becoming increasingly restless with their raising thoughts as manifested in the intellectual, atmospheric pressure of Pacland forums and other auxiliaries.

After all the rousing days and short intermittent sleeping hours leading to this day, I walk semi-dazed from the parking lot into the MGM Grand still thinking that all boxing prophets must make arguments, regardless of whether they be rhetorical, direct persuasion or simply a false notion. Rightly so, when I set out to think about boxing, I must not hesitate to use the written word to lend humanity to this brutal craft. As of this writing, I sense something that others may otherwise be expecting: Cotto must have felt his time, if not his career, slipping away!

If you observe the countenance of Cotto as he edges into the fight night with Pacquiao, you would say his is not similar to the image of Moses at Mount Sinai and does not even come close to that of Pacquiao. Much more, Cotto's image today is different from the all-too-familiar pre-fight mode of the "Miguel Cotto" of yesteryears.

Yes, Cotto's bearing has been reduced to that of a "below-the-belt" albeit still hard-hitting, hopeless "Pharaoh" whose insistence of unbelief and willful intent to hold the Israelites in bondage to slavery brought him an even more devastating defeat at the hands of the Creative Force of the Universe. Cotto finds his best comfort from the meditations of his solitude, enslaving himself with inelastic fortitude during his training. . .least of himself becoming a headhunter for tonight's fight, dubbed "Fire Power" here at the MGM Grand Arena.

But, Pacquiao says it otherwise: "Don't bother Cotto about being too serious; he wants to become a religious person." Pacquiao says it playfully in front of the media personalities and some fans standing elbow to elbow along the ropes of the ring inside the Wild Card Gym during the "open work out" for media last week.

Indeed, Cotto has all the reasons to be dead serious. He is facing a smaller, but skillful man, who is more charismatic and popular than he. This, despite the fact that Cotto is regarded as one of the greatest athletes Puerto Rico has ever had. After all, other than the honorary WBC Diamond Belt, he must feel it a bit odd to be the underdog even though his own WBO Welterweight Championship belt is on the line for the contest.

Cotto may not be the same fighter who fought Judah, Mosley, Clottey, Margarito and the rest of the victims. But, one thing for sure, he would still be the same dirty fighter who fought Torres in 2005. And that's where his basic instinct shines, especially when the going gets tough.

Conversely, forget about the game plans and power that catapulted him to the series of victories that he is known for. He only has his lone, questionable defeat from Antonio Margarito, who may have used illegal hand wraps during their fight. He has better game plans and much greater power than his previous fights. He is ready to present surprises which may not be conceivable to Pacquiao fans. He is bound to do anything he can to get the nods from at least two of the three judges, namely: Adalaide Byrd, Duane Ford and Dave Moretti. Not to forget referee Kenny Bayless and the ring physicians, whose technical decisions will critically come into play.

I must extrapolate this again from my previous article: Cotto is better than those scripted scenes from HBO's 24/7 episodes. And take this: I vouch his jabs may throw off Pacquiao's timing especially in the first two rounds. And with Pacquiao's attempts to inflict four to five combos, Cotto is likely to mix up his uppercuts and may try to dig inside, which would somehow give Pacquiao a bit of a problem.

But Pacquiao's straight left may send Cotto fewer nerve signals in a way that he would feel it as more fatal than Margarito's illegal wraps, even in the second or third round if there's more time left. I see what I saw in Cotto versus Judah wherein Cotto had problems with Judah's straight left. But, most of all, one thing is clear here: Pacquiao has better stamina than Judah. And Cotto would find this insurmountable because of Pacquiao's inherent hand speed and unpredictable footwork. But, Cotto would do anything he could to survive round 4.

If one wants to see the true Cotto, then it is his fight against Ricardo Torres in 2005 that must be worth-focusing. Torres got his worth in the arms of Cotto in the first round with an initial knockdown and then Cotto got his in the mind of Torres who kept coming forward with bomb after bomb and dropped him in round 2 after taking voluminous shots to the body and upstairs. And watch Cotto's deliberate quick shot to the left thigh of Torres as he delivered a series of combos and sucked up Torres' unrelenting advances in the same round.

Then, with the intention of favorably affecting deeper inflammatory processes to Torres's right thigh and lower abdominal quadrant, Cotto successfully fired five to six low-blows in the 3rd round, right before the eyes of referee Dave Fields.

Yes, Fields must have lost his mind, as if he was watching a sexual act. . .just having his eyes fixed, if not suspended at the ill-doings of Cotto in many instances. Or, he just lacked sleep from his previous night outings. In fact, Cotto held his composure and still deliberately dug another low blow, causing a knockdown in the 4th. Torres was clearly the better fighter on that night, if not the spoiling, fatigue-inducing low blows of Cotto.

Yes, it was a night adulterated by the worst referee and the dirtiest fighter ever. But, as for Pacquiao versus Cotto, Pacquiao's style of a fighting cock Kelso would make Pacquiao appear illusive, yes. . .elusive as well. Meanwhile, what took place in Cotto versus Torres should not have a repeat tonight. Referee Kenny Bayless should render a drastic measure, if the same incidents happen. Time and again, Cotto would just say: "I am not Ricky Hatton. I am not Oscar de la Hoya. I am Miguel Cotto."

TECTONIC SHIFT CONTINUES

POUND-FOR-POUND KING MANNY "PACMAN" PACQUIAO STILL REIGNS AND WINS BOTH THE WBO WELTERWEIGHT CHAMPIONSHIP AND THE FIRST-EVER HONORARY WBC DIAMOND BELTS BY STOPPAGE IN THE FINAL ROUND.

NOVEMBER 14, 2009: MGM GRAND ARENA, LAS VEGAS, NEVADA – The raucous crowd of 15,535 took their moments of madness with their voices in crescendo into a blockbuster haste as two great men pressed on time busting up to stamp their respective might in the annals of history in boxing.

But, one man stole the hearts of many and even now still strikes awe: Manny "Pacman" Pacquiao of the Philippines. Pacquiao, the Pound-for-Pound king of boxing, cranked up his masterstroke of boxing skills over reigning WBO Welterweight Champion Miguel Cotto of Puerto Rico, whose title was on the line along with the first-ever honorary WBC Diamond Championship Belt and became the first boxer to have won seven titles in seven weight divisions.

As Pacquiao revved up and accelerated his strength to put forth Cotto into submission in the final round, Referee Bayless aborted the bout while the former mounted a series of landed shots to the head at 55 seconds from the opening bell. It was a tumultuous moment for Cotto. Bayless just made it right when he halted the fight at such a moment on the 20' x 20' canvas of MGM Grand Arena, which the world was anxious to see. Cotto shares with Pacquiao the unforgotten moments that cannot be forcibly erased from his memory – moments which he must wish to bury in order to deny the brutality of boxing it offers.

Morphing into an unrepentant and "hopeless Pharaoh," Cotto angled his sight digging repeated low-blows in round one, two and four. Indeed, Cotto held his ground in the first round, countering Pacquiao's straight lefts which gave a bit of trouble to the Maharlikan hero.

Left hook to the body and one right uppercut to the chin snapped back Pacquiao's head. Such signaled Pacquiao to be more calculating with his frontal attacks. In fact, he stroke back with right hooks but missed his targets.

Round 2 shifted to more jabs of Cotto in the opening. But Pacquiao took hold of his guard and launched effective combos, putting Cotto in puzzled mode from his opponent's speed and increasing accuracy. His nasal bridge turned red. And – that's right – still unrepentant! Cotto promptly resorted to his basic instinct: his arsenals of digging low-blows which landed and sweeping head butts which failed to crush on.

From round 2 through 4, Pacquiao surged to another level. While vicious combinations failed to stop Cotto's countering uppercuts, Pacquiao playfully allowed Cotto to land body shots while he was leaning on the ropes at times, blocking his face from potential shots upstairs. Testing his guard, Pacquiao encouraged Cotto to engage more and then the heavy exchanges turned the attendees' thunderous chanting into insanity.

And so the tectonic left bolted in round 3 with a knockdown that shook Cotto's senses. Nonetheless, Cotto kept his advances with counter-punching, one of which snapped back Pacquiao's head again to the thin air of madness.

The crowd never stopped chanting "Manny, Manny, Manny. . ." with a sporadic countering of "Cotto, Cotto, Cotto. . ." as the two warriors fought each other back and forth in rapid succession. Then, Pacquiao surged again to a much higher level, which was manifested by him making a sign of the cross just when each bell rang. And, Pacquiao dropped Cotto again from a quick left uppercut in round 4.

Tectonic Shift Continues

Round 5 brought a tide of virtually divided cheering at irregular beats and Pacquiao appeared to be closing the scene of brutality as he delivered intensive surgical attacks that somehow intercepted the timing of Cotto's punches. Bomb after bomb exploded from bilateral jabs and uppercuts. But Cotto started to refuse to strike a toe-to-toe combat and engaged instead in a dancing retreat in the fashion of the Old Taino Indians of Puerto Rico – retreating in fact, like a bleeding bull but still with willful intent to retaliate all the way to the final round.

Despite his setbacks and the likelihood of getting knocked out, Cotto deferred the suggestion of his trainer, Joe Santiago, to give up the fight in the eleventh. Cotto chose otherwise, hoping to catch an opening for a one-punch knockout, or finish up the night with 12 rounds of boxing.

In due course at exactly 55 seconds from the opening of the final round, Referee Bayless saw it timely to stop the fight after Manny unloaded heavy shots to the swollen and crimson red face of Cotto, notwithstanding the neurovascular shots to the head that twice put Cotto in momentary stupor by the rope.

Cotto landed single digits in power shots from the fifth through the twelfth round, throwing 597 punches, of which only 172 connected. Pacquiao, on the other hand, threw 780, out of which 336 landed. Jabs thrown by Cotto were 227, of which 79 connected versus of Pacquiao, 220, out of which 60 connected. Total power punches thrown by Cotto were 300, of which 93 connected versus of Pacquiao, 560, of which 276 landed.

Status Post Fight:

Cotto kept his composure at ease despite his brutal defeat at the hands of the Maharlikan hero. "Pacquiao is one of the best boxers in the world," said Cotto in the post fight interview just before he was brought to a nearby hospital for brain scans and for other medical protocol to be observed. "I am amazed at his speed. I didn't see many of his punches coming, but they were landing harder and harder."

"I thought I was going to control the fight from round 1 and the rest of the rounds, but he surprised me with big combinations," Cotto said while his escorts were leading him out of the arena to his convenience room to ready for ambulance transport.

Asked if he intended to fight again, Cotto said, "I want to have a vacation with my family and I will let Bob Arum to decide my next fight." Cotto's utterances upon his defeat told a lot of a humble man. He was not defensive of his shortcomings.

Meanwhile, Joe Santiago, Cotto's trainer, said his "boxer had a tremendous heart." In fact, "he made it a fight with Pacquiao despite the fact he got cuts and bloody and he was retreating in the later rounds but still had capability to strike back."

"I admire Cotto's courage." Santiago said. "He is a great boxer."

Yes, Pacquiao said good points of Cotto's courage: "Cotto is a very respectful person and he is a tough fighter and a good boxer." In fact, "I had difficulty adjusting to his counter-punching in the early rounds," Pacquiao explained as he tugged the tip of his black French hat on the top of his bandage near his right temple, which was protecting his bleeding right ear canal. Pacquiao said further: "In the first three rounds, I was trying to measure his power."

Other than head-snapping uppercuts, Pacquiao took several head shots as well to both lateral sides. "I got hurt, too, but I was just pretending that I did not get hurt," he chuckled, adding, "Cotto is a strong puncher."Asked to compare himself with other boxers, Pacquiao said: "I do not want to compare myself with anybody."

But one thing is clear: Pacquiao had an edge over Cotto. Pacquiao also has an anointed Master. "Now, I call him: Master Freddie Roach," Pacquiao declared before over 300 media personnel and VIP's in the media center.

In Pacquiao's brief speech other than the interviews, Pacquiao said: "I was just doing my job. My goal is to give happiness to people." But Freddie Roach, the celebrated trainer, thought otherwise. He said: "You're the greatest fighter of this era." Pacquiao responded: "Sorry, Master. . ." He was referring to his refusal to acknowledge his greatness before the media, reminding him that he is just a fighter who does his job in the ring."

Tectonic Shift Continues

Asked as to how he felt about the fight with Cotto, Pacquiao said: "I think this is one of the toughest fights in my career." Asked once more about what he was thinking from the start of the fight, Pacquiao said: "Be smart in the fight and control the fight" and ". . .pretending I didn't get hurt, but it really hurts"(sic).

Pacquiao closed his brief appearance at the post fight conference with an invitation to attend his concert costing $ 40 per person. He did not hesitate to tell the media personalities to pay the price, in that he said he will have his renditions of eight songs.

Asked by the media to let them hear a sample, Pacquiao exuded a flashy shift singing three lines of his favorite song which he sang at the Jimmy Kimmel Live Show: "Sometimes When We Touch". And so the tectonic shift continues.

MAYWEATHER JR. AND PACQUIAO STILL INDISPENSABLE TO EACH OTHER'S GLORY?

MAY 21, 2010: HOLLYWOOD, CALIFORNIA – Of the two great warriors and the immortality of boxing from the sundown of each Saturday, ring controversies divide writers and fans alike over misconceptions. While one fighter lays the foundation of aggression the other projects a less offensive but tactical play only to slide and evade from danger and to counter-attack.

The same fighters may have nearly the same fearless might at some level, especially during their 'fight or flight' response. Together we ask: Who is really indispensable to one's glory and who is the No. 1 boxer of this era?

This question can be puzzling at length, especially when a boxing fan believes himself as persuasive, given all the logic and expletives he has at his own disposal. But, there can be a reason for lack of persuasiveness. One is likely to begin that Mayweather, Jr. fights better than Pacquiao. Whether that understanding is applied fairly, and whether it deters further argument, depends upon who takes that proposition seriously. In a lighter vein, the perspective of a layman in the understanding of boxers' rising popularity must be examined. A case in point is about Pacquiao's imminence to become a household name in the U.S. and his explosive, even rising popularity over Mayweather, Jr.'s prominence in penetrating the American market.

And this, as the author hopes, should suffice one's appetite for learning, much more in the debates of the sweet science of boxing as to whether Floyd Mayweather, Jr. really still reigns as the Pound-for-Pound king of boxing. Let us start with the statistical breakdown of my premise from a recent survey, which is done every five years by the United States Bureau of Census. The U.S. population's distribution by race and ethnicity in 2010 was as follows:

Total population:

- United States: 309,321,088
- World: 6,822,346,568

Disparity of Entries in Weight Classes versus Market Penetration and Segmentation:

Where was Pacquiao at the height of Mayweather's popularity in the U.S.? Mayweather launched his first professional fight at 130 pounds in 1996 a few months before he turned 20 while Pacquiao fought his first professional debut in the Philippines at 107 pounds just when he was about to turn 17 in 1995.

And while Mayweather, Jr. won his first championship belt (WBC Super Featherweight), from Gerraro Hernandez in 1998 after the latter's fifth title defense at 130 pounds in the U.S., Manny Pacquiao also won in the same year his first world title, WBC Flyweight belt, of which he slugged it out from Chatchai Sasakul via TKO in round 8 at 112 pounds in Thailand.

Then, after losing the same title in 1999 to Medgoen Singsurat by TKO in round 3, Pacquiao went on to fight for the WBC International Super Bantamweight title against Reynante Jamili and won TKO in round 2. So, one could see during which time Mayweather was already soaking the American market even before he won the National Golden Gloves Light Flyweight Championship in 1993. Mayweather was on his way to winning the Featherweight Bronze Medal for the U.S. at the Olympics in Atlanta in 1996 while Pacquiao was just soaking the Asian market, outside of the U.S. and literally has not touched the American market not until 2001.

And so Pacquiao fought thereafter five defenses before he launched his first U.S. debut against Lehlohonolo Ledwaba in 2001 and won the IBF Super Bantamweight title at 122 pounds via brutal knockout in the sixth, during which time Mayweather had just snatched the WBC Super Featherweight Championship belt from Diego Corrales at 130 pounds by TKO in round 10.

Now, let us think about the demographics of the U.S. from 2006, at least roughly with minimal margin of errors as to the historical percentages by ethnicity. Other than Caucasians and Latinos, African-American remains the dominant race in the sports arenas through which Mayweather's name has attained an almost perfect "name-recall" in every family of African descent, free-riding over the famous black boxers such as Muhammed Ali, Joe Frazer, George Forman, Sugar Ray Leonard and Mike Tyson, notwithstanding retired British boxer and undisputed World Heavyweight Champion Lennox Lewis who eventually migrated to the United States.

Banking on those 2006 statistical data, matching Mayweather with any of the famous Mexican boxers such as Manuel Marquez or Julio Ceasar Chavez, Jr. would bring a deeper awakening penetration at a greater percentage of the Latino's 44.3 million population in the United States.

Yes, despite Mayweather's flawless professional record of forty fights, he is by far seen as the reigning "controversial boxing" hero in the African-American community, which has an explosive population of 40.9 million in the U.S., according to the United States Bureau of Census' statistical survey in 2006.

Consider this: Matching a superstar fighter from one of the top ethnic groups with another would only need to sway 3% of their respective ethnic population to make the fight a blockbuster. You see, Mayweather would only need to "soak the beans" over a few nights to get his own turf's attention despite his behavioral issues. In fact, he only needs to verbalize a few nasty words to get under the skin of the Latinos, to stimulate tremendous market demand from such segment.

All the Latino fans can continually hope to see Mayweather getting knocked out by a Latino boxer, as in the case of Mayweather vs. Marquez. The prospect of jubilance is what they yearn for, all because of that magnifying power of "La Raza". . . that sense of pride, that state of deprivation in uplifting the ego of the psyche of a "Me-xi-ca-no."

And Mayweather does not need to know the psychology of this game. In fact, that is deeply embedded in his own fiber. As for Pacquiao, it is the rare force of nature in him that really spells out the difference. His God-given ability to capture the hearts of boxing fans called "charisma" and his willful, unrelenting drive to fight to the end inclusive of his increasing knockout power, all make a compelling, total package of an inspirational fighter, notwithstanding his simple, humble words he uses to describe status-post each of his fights.

On one hand, targeting a specific marketing niche is not an easy game for many local fighters. How much more for a foreign fighter whose last name was unknown to the general boxing public in 2001, which may somehow qualify for insertion as a text in the tongue twister of "Peter Piper picked a peck of pickled peppers. . ." by Mother Goose, or that which some Americans even mispronounce as, "Pac-U." Such last name, "Pacquiao," cannot easily sink down into the "molecules" of the American brain.

Never forget: Pacquiao is reaching his target market in a seemingly wider range, even at a grander scale, as manifested on the front cover of Time Magazine and his appearances in hot TV shows in the U.S., breaking the walls of cultural and racial indifference. Pacquiao has his genuine fans in every ethnic group, symbolic of a phenomenal metamorphosis of his international appeal to this racially divided land of milk and honey.

But whether Mayweather still captures the hearts of his African-American community and even the quasi ones is a question that really does not need legal jargon to win. He is still well-loved as Pretty Boy, even to the point spoiling his conduct into unbecoming of a respectable man in the public eye.

Meanwhile, the fact that Pacquiao has penetrated the American market even unto the halls of Hollywood celebrities makes him phenomenal than Mayweather's egotistical, much less paradoxical, mythical command that he claims.

After all, it only needs the layman's view to distinguish these two fighters, whether one is for pay-per-view sales or for the interest of the boxing fans. Last November 14, Pacquiao versus Cotto did not just get at least one million PPV sales. Such a day was void of any national day for both countries: Puerto Rico and Philippines. There was commonality here between these two roots: Puerto Ricans and Filipinos were likely to watch "Fire Power" in a party of at least seven in a family, plus friends. Cotto versus Pacquiao would be in no way at par to pull out better PPV sales, if such fight depended only from these two ethnic groups.

Nevertheless, Pacquiao has gone deeper in penetrating mainstream America regardless of ethnic backgrounds. As retired U.S. lawyer William Jasper said, "Manny Pacquiao has got what it takes to recapture the American hearts into sweet science of boxing."

Unlike Mayweather's magnetism, Pacquiao's phenomenal appeal in view of market segmentation should not be studied in the pre-text of the U.S. demographics but in the context of international scene simply because he is a foreign fighter with increasingly broader base of American and trans-racial fans than what Mayweather has, so to speak.

Take a look at the figures Pacquiao versus Clottey had spawned at the Dallas Cowboys Stadium in Arlington, Texas. Over 51,000 attendees put in an estimated $4.9 million in gross gate sales despite Clottey's less convincing appeal to the American market since his impressive win against Jeffrey Hill, whom he knocked him out in round 6 at the Crown Plaza in New York in 2003, and onward. The demographics in Arlington, Texas simply represent mainstream America: less of minorities and mostly Caucasians. Nonetheless, Pacquiao had the commanding appeal of "The Event."

Let us check the statistics of other boxing events below as provided by the Nevada Athletic Commission:

NEVADA'S LARGEST GROSSING GATES

The top 36 categorized by main event, venue, promoter, date of the event, paid attendance and gross sales:

1. FLOYD MAYWEATHER JR vs. OSCAR DE LA HOYA
   MGM, Golden Boy, Don Chargin, PPV 05/05/07 - 17,078 - $18,419,200.00

2. LENNOX LEWIS vs. EVANDER HOLYFIELD II
   Thomas and Mack, Don King, PPV 11/13/99 - 17,078 - $16,860,300.00

3. EMMANUEL PACQUIAO vs. OSCAR DE LA HOYA
   MGM, Golden Boy, Top Rank, PPV 12/06/08 - 14,468 - $14,380,300.00

4. EVANDER HOLYFIELD vs. MIKE TYSON II
   MGM, Don King, PPV 06/28/97 - 16,279 - $14,277,200.00

5. EVANDER HOLYFIELD vs. MIKE TYSON I
   MGM, Don King, PPV 11/09/96 - 16,103 - $14,150,700.00

6. MIKE TYSON vs. PETER MC NEELEY
   MGM, Don King, PPV 08/19/95 - 16,113 - $13,965,600.00

7. FELIX TRINIDAD vs. OSCAR DE LA HOYA
   Mandalay Bay, Top Rank, Don King, PPV 09/18/99 - 11,184 - $12,949,500.00

8. BERNARD HOPKINS vs. OSCAR DE LA HOYA
   MGM, Top Rank, Golden Boy, PPV 09/18/04 - 15,672 - $12,782,650.00

9. JOE CALZAGHE vs. BERNARD HOPKINS
   Thomas & Mack, Golden Boy, Don Chargin, HBO 04/19/08 14,345 - $11,636,400.00

10. FLOYD MAYWEATHER JR vs. SHANE MOSLEY
    MGM, Golden Boy, Don Chargin, PPV 05/01/10 - 14,038 - $11,032,100.00

11. MIKE TYSON vs. FRANK BRUNO II
    MGM, Don King, PPV 03/16/96 - 16,143 - $10,673,700.00

12. FLOYD MAYWEATHER JR vs. RICKY HATTON
    MGM, Golden Boy, PPV - 12/08/07 - 15,488 - $10,393,950.00

13. SHANE MOSLEY vs. OSCAR DE LA HOYA
    MGM, Top Rank, PPV 09/13/03 - 16,074 - $9,840,000.00

14. OSCAR DE LA HOYA vs. FERNANDO VARGAS
    Mandalay Bay, Top Rank, PPV 09/14/02 - 10,984 - $8,871,300.00

15. EMMANUEL PACQUIAO vs. MIGUEL ANGEL COTTO
    MGM, Golden Boy, Top Rank, PPV 11/14/09 15,470 - $8,847,550.00

16. EMMANUEL PACQUIAO vs. RICHARD HATTON
    MGM, Golden Boy, Top Rank, PPV 05/02/09 -15,368 - $8,832,950.00

17. OSCAR DE LA HOYA vs. RICARDO MAYORGA
    MGM, Golden Boy, Don King, Don Chargin, PPV 05/06/06 - 12,276 - $7,636,000.00

18. OSCAR DE LA HOYA vs. JULIO C. CHAVEZ I
    Caesars Palace, Top Rank, Don King, Close Circuit 06/07/96 - 14,738 - $7,579,100.00

19. LENNOX LEWIS vs. HASIM RAHMAN
    Mandalay Bay, Don King, Main Events, Lion, PPV 11/17/01 -9,830 - $7,537,400.00

20. FELIX TRINIDAD vs. FERNANDO VARGAS
Mandalay Bay, Don King, Main Events, PPV 12/02/00 -9,309 - $7,486,400.00

21. FELIX TRINIDAD vs. DAVID REID
Caesars Palace, Don King, America Presents, PPV 03/03/00 -9,584 - $7,329,500.00

22. MIKE TYSON vs. FRANCOIS BOTHA
MGM, America Presents, PPV 01/16/99 - 10,221 - $7,055,800.00

23. EVANDER HOLYFIELD vs. JAMES DOUGLAS
Mirage, Mirage, PPV 10/25/90 - 10,117 - $6,546,441.00

24. ROY JONES JR vs. JOHN RUIZ
Mirage, Mirage, PPV 03/01/03 - 11,490 - $6,526,350.00

25. LENNOX LEWIS vs. DAVID TUA
Mandalay Bay, Main Events, America Presents, Panix, PPV 11/11/00- 10,809 -$6,508,500.00

26. RAY LEONARD vs. THOMAS HEARNS II
Caesars Palace, Top Rank, PPV 06/12/89 -12,064 - $6,468,600.00

27. RAY LEONARD vs. ROBERTO DURAN
Mirage, Top Rank, Victory Promotions, PPV 12/07/89 - 11,904 - $6,448,700.00

28. RONALD "WINKY" WRIGHT vs. FELIX TRINIDAD
MGM, Don King, Gary Shaw, Guilty, PPV 05/14/05 - 13,590 - $6,433,500.00

29. MIKE TYSON vs. BRUCE SELDON
MGM, Don King, PPV 09/07/96 - 9,511 - $6,305,900.00

30. **LARRY HOLMES vs. GERRY COONEY
    Caesars Palace, Don King, Tiffany, Close Circuit 06/11/82 - 29,214 **Also highest attendance - $6,239,050.00

31. RAY LEONARD vs. MARVIN HAGLER
    Caesars Palace, Top Rank, Victory Promotions, Close Circuit 04/06/87 - 12,379 - $6,215,400.00

32. MIKE TYSON vs. DONOVAN RUDDOCK II
    Mirage, Don King, 3M Productions, PPV 06/28/91 - 13,047 - $6,200,276.50

33. EVANDER HOLYFIELD vs. RIDDICK BOWE II
    Caesars Palace, Spencer Promotions, Main Events, PPV 11/06/93 - 10,923 - $5,792,838.50

34. LARRY HOLMES vs. MUHAMMAD ALI
    Caesars Palace, Don King, NBC 10/02/80 24,570 - $5,766,125.00

35. EVANDER HOLYFIELD vs. MICHAEL MOORER
    Thomas & Mack, Mirage, Don King, Main Events, Fight Night, PPV 11/08/97 - 9,395 - $5,566,700.00

36. MIKE TYSON vs. DONOVAN RUDDOCK I
    Mirage, Don King, 3M Productions, PPV 03/18/91 - 12,563 - $5,454,918.50

Remember, mentioned above are gross sales at gates as supplied through the Nevada Athletic Commission.

Conversely, one of the reasons why both fights of Mayweather, Jr. against Marquez and Mosley did well in gross sales is because the strategic focus of their respective campaigns was rather extrinsic in value: the frequent use of the name of Pacquiao in any interview or in every HBO episode to stimulate interests from the boxing public and to elicit their buying power even for an unmerited spending.

What most boxing fans want to see would be a knockout loss of Mayweather, Jr. to either opponent. Mayweather and his villainous aura truly ignite the boxing public to watch him fight, win or lose. But, Mayweather's 12-round decision victory on May 1 in Las Vegas drew 1.4 million domestic buys, worth about $78.3 million in revenue.

Pacquiao's bout with Ghana's Joshua Clottey attracted a total of 700,000 pay-per-view buys translating to $35.3 million in domestic television revenue plus estimated $4.9 million in gross gate sales, according to Top Rank Godfather Bob Arum, which total is less of what the Mayweather, Jr.-Mosley fight drew.

According to a report by *ESPN.com*, the figures were disclosed by Mark Taffet of HBO PPV, which aired the Pacquiao-Clottey fight live from the famed Cowboys Stadium in Arlington, Texas, last March 14.

As of this writing, the public eye in the world of boxing sees Pacquiao as having that innate power and distinctive ability to defeat, if not knock out, Mayweather in the ring of violence. But, does Pacquiao really need Mayweather at this stage of his career? In other words, is Mayweather still indispensable for Pacquiao's glory, vice versa? Maybe not! Of course, at 31, Pacquiao must look forward to better health and healing than just hungering for more in the realm of ring violence.

Nonetheless, Pacquiao being a elected to the 15th Congress of the Philippines representing Sarangani, he might still be tempted to take a final shot against Juan Manuel Marquez in the full-welterweight limit, not catch-weight, if not against Mayweather. This can be a momentous appeal before the world stage of boxing to have a congressman-elect fighting again for the welfare of his people, however dishonorable it may be. After all, the promises he has made to build a hospital and a university in Sarangani may not come to pass. Pork barrel allocation for that said district may not be enough to finance Pacquiao's lofty plans. Making a comeback just before he makes it official to have his door closed for boxing may just be the only way to set his lips from being laden with promise and hope. Yes, Pacquiao needs to fight once more, all for the sake of Sarangani.

For the Land of Promise, Mindanao, Pacquiao may have to fulfill his lofty aims through his sweat of blood and higher scale of pain in the land of milk and honey. One farewell fight is not bad at all, at least for all his fans as well. Sure, he'll be missed. Whether you like it not, Pacquiao has successfully invaded the progressively insurmountable segment of the American market. The trend is that Pacquiao's popularity constantly goes up while Mayweather's constantly declines faster than you think.

Take it or leave it: Pacquiao, indeed, is the Pound-for-Pound King! As for Mayweather, Jr. and in fairness to his drawing power, he is the true Pay-per-View King!

PACMAN CHECKMATES THE GRANDMASTER

MARCH 13, 2010: RINGSIDE REPORT FROM DALLAS COWBOY STADIUM, ARLINGTON, TEXAS - Pacquiao retains his WBO Welterweight title after unanimously gaining a decision victory over the tough panther of Ghana, Joshua "Grand Master" Clottey. In the early rounds through the ninth, Clottey kept his defense tight and was more reluctant to openly engage Pacquiao's non-stop aggression. Fiery shots that mostly landed on the gloves and blocked by the forearms of Clottey never stopped the latter from moving forward.

But Pacquiao's surgical, abdominal body shots heavily landed, mostly on the left quadrant and a few to the right and mid-section as Clottey pressed on his defenses. "I lost this fight with Manny," Clottey said of Pacquiao who threw more jabs in the first round making it the highest number of jabs he had thrown of his entire boxing career. "I did my best. But, Manny is fast."

For the twelve rounds, Pacquiao threw 1,231 punches, landing 246 while Clottey landed 108 out of 399, showing the latter a much higher rate of accuracy. But, Pacquiao threw 682 power punches versus Clottey's 237.

Clottey said, "He is extremely fast. That's the best thing about him...his speed." One judge scored every round for Pacquiao while the two gave round 3 to Clottey, giving Pacquiao a unanimous decision victory. In that victorious third round for Clottey, he launched two counter-attacks, of which he landed one to the forehead, another to the face and a distinguishing uppercut which snapped back the head of Pacquiao.

As manifested by Pacquiao's frustration over Clottey's insistence not to engage proactively and exchange leathers from the first through mid-rounds, Pacquiao, as well, made a sweeping record as the first fighter who fired Clottey with bilateral hands hammering simultaneously the temporal sides in the fourth round, prompting the referee to give him a warning of such illegal shots.

The fifth round marked the point wherein Clottey started to attack Pacquiao sporadically. One uppercut had Pacquiao's head snapped back again, which the former again successfully landed in the seventh. But the latter retaliated with body shots and more jabs upstairs, mostly blocked, even in the eighth and onward.

Clottey showed himself as the aggressor right after the bell rang in the tenth and got Pacquiao with an uppercut and three more sharp uppercuts in the eleventh. All were met by the latter's persistent counter-attacks, gunning a barrage of punches that almost sent the former to the canvas.

In the final found, Manny Pacquiao took a deep breath, looked straight to Clottey, and stared up high and made a sign of the cross – a kind of belief in a transcendent reality he invokes each time he fights, as the twelfth round of boxing was about to start.

But, as they met in the center of the ring they both hugged each other as the thunderous cheers of over 51,000 in attendance reverberated in the $1.3 billion facility of gigantic proportion. Then, the final event took the stand. Both fighters were equally active. But, Pacquiao landed more power shots after an accidental clash of heads in the middle of the round.

And it went through with both fighters finishing the bout fresh and strong as if three more rounds were needed to re-establish a comparative historic mark of 15 rounds back to the times of Muhammad "The Greatest" Ali, Joe Frazier and Leon Spinks.

Asked if Pacquiao hurt him with some of the big shots, Clottey said: "I was not hurt at all." Pacquiao thought Clottey is a very strong fighter. "I tried my very best for a knockout but Clottey is a very strong fighter and has a very good defense," said Pacquiao on his way to the locker room along with his escorts.

Conversely, some fans wanted Pacquiao, who is running for Congress in the lone district of Sarangani this May 13, 2010 in the Philippine National Elections, to fight again. Others hoped he will not. "I hope this will be the last fight for Pacquiao. Otherwise, he will face the same fate of Muhammad Ali who lost to undefeated Larry Holmes by referee technical decision in round 10 and to Trevor Berbick by unanimous decision, both beat him badly after his glorious bout against Leon Spinks in 1978," said Jeff Reeves, one of Pacquiao's fans who drove from Michigan just to watch "The Event" live.

But, most sportswriters, including this author, and most fans, still hope the Mayweather-Pacquiao fight will happen before the close of this year. And Pacquiao himself wanted the fight as well. "I want that fight, but it's up to him. I am ready to fight anytime," said Pacquiao. "Maybe if Mosley wins, I'll fight him," Pacquiao said before the match between Mosley and Mayweather on May 1, 2010 at the MGM Grand Arena in Las Vegas, Nevada. Both Top Rank Godfather Bob Arum and the celebrated trainer of Pacquiao, Freddie Roach, wanted either fighters to fight Pacquiao based on whoever wins their match. "I want to see Floyd Mayweather, Jr. getting knocked out by Pacquiao and it's going to happen," said Roach. "I don't want to hear any excuses from him."

On the other hand, Arum remained apprehensive of the tactical play the Mayweather camp will employ relative to extraneous issues on drug testing by a series of random blood draws inside 30 days of the fight date. "The issue of drug testing is not for one fighter to raise in negotiations. It doesn't belong there," Arum said. "There are applicable people who are charged with a policy of administering items like drug testing."

"We believe that Floyd Mayweather, Jr. raised that issue to duck Manny Pacquiao," Arum added.

Meanwhile, Jerry Jones, owner of the Dallas Cowboy Stadium, expects another fight of Pacquiao to happen this year. "It's been an ambition of mine and an ambition of ours to have a great fighter of Pacquiao's stature to fight with another great fighter here in Dallas Cowboys Stadium again this year," said Jones. "This is an amazing history for all of us. I am very happy of the outcome, and it helps the stadium to easily promote future boxing events," Jones added.

Pacquiao, 31, improves 51 wins inclusive of 38 knockouts, 3 losses and 2 draws while Clottey, 32, scores 35 wins inclusive of 20 knockouts, with 3 losses, of which the latter maintains zero knockout loss as against the former with 2 knockout losses, of their respective entire boxing careers.

5 MARGARITO MISCONCEPTIONS

YAHOO! SPORTS - NOVEMBER 14, 2010 AT 8:00 A.M.: ARLINGTON, TEXAS - Tensions between Emmanuel "Pacman" Pacquiao and Antonio "Tornado" Margarito still progressively run higher as the day of judgment in the ring of madness nears its consummation.

They will have to square-off for boxing's WBC Super Welterweight Title on November 13, 2010, this Saturday, at the Dallas Cowboy Stadium in Arlington, Texas. But regardless of the intensity of the tensions between these two contending forces, the pervading misconceptions about Margarito rob off the boxing aficionados and fans' expectations come fight night.

Here are the top five misconceptions, to wit:

1. Margarito being tall must stand taller than Pacquiao on fight night: Just because Margarito is 5 inches taller than Pacquiao does not mean his height is an "automatic natural defense factor"; meaning, he would just be less active than what Pacquiao must do. Having such height advantage is a plus only if Margarito can mount a good physical defense and also able to maximize his reach and compete with the speed of Pacquiao, not necessarily faster than him but at least close enough to deter quick hammering attacks.

2. Margarito, though in top form, lacks compelling power over Pacquiao: While the suspicion still pervades in the minds of some boxing aficionados and fans that Margarito may have used at the height of his popularity the same kind of "Plaster of Paris" that which he got caught just before he fought on the fight night against Mosley, Pacquiao should not underestimate the margin of error of these thinkers. If they had to build their arguments, as per assessments, from Margarito's last two fights with Mosley and Roberto Garcia, then they must be completely wrong. And that does not exclude the presumptive analysis by Freddie Roach, Pacquiao's trainer, that Margarito had just relied all his power punches from that illegal hand wraps which "unknowingly" was about to be used as a weapon against Mosley.

3. Margarito lacks the ability to duplicate Buster Douglas, a 50-1 underdog at the time, who scored a tenth-round knockout against the previously undefeated Mike Tyson in February 1990: The odds-makers must be concerned. History, whether it is in sports or other venues of life, is replete with surprises. Another example, most people were shocked when a relatively unknown Cassius Clay (who later changed his name to Muhammad Ali) defeated the big hitter Sonny Liston for the heavyweight title in 1964. Another surprise came when Leon Spinks took the title away from Ali on a split decision in 1978. What about a 45-year old George Foreman who knocked out Michael Moorer in 10 rounds in 1994? What about Evander Holyfield who was a heavy underdog when he beat Mike Tyson on an eleventh-round technical knockout in 1996.

4. Margarito lacks the skill to mount a "rope-a-dope" boxing strategy to tire out Pacquiao and launch a full-scale attack in later rounds: No matter how predictable Margarito is in the sight of Pacquiao, an element of difficulty in maneuvering Margarito may still exist. If Margarito can employ this tactic against a stronger, though smaller and shorter fighter in Pacquiao, then laying back against the ropes and waiting for the opponent to tire himself out, and then taking advantage of Pacquiao's exhaustion can be a great advantage for him, only if he has that tremendous ability to take the punishment that Pacquiao could dish out.

5. Margarito lacks considerable defense and ability to use his jabs accurately toward a fast-moving target: This can be a big factor since Margarito is a lot slower than Pacquiao. Chasing a mouse but not finding it is not a good game at all; nor throwing but not quite landing, or striking but not quite hard enough. Antonio Margarito, being a less respected figure among the great fighters of Mexican bloodlines, will have a bearing of a life-size icon in himself to which his fans, the underworld and even the hoodlums, may indulge his power and authority in the ring for a potential win over the best boxer of the planet, Emmanuel "Pacman" Pacquiao of the Philippines.

TOP PAY-PER-VIEW BOXING EVENTS AS OF MAY 2012

*B*ig boxing matches surprise us by landing thumping lefts and rights with big names such as Manny Pacquiao, Oscar De La Hoya, Mike Tyson, Muhammed Ali, Floyd Mayweather, Jr., Evander Holyfield, Felix Trinidad, Lennox Lewis and more. But who really are the top-notchers among them in the pay-per-view (PPV) buys?

Rather, it's tough to find a definitive top ten list qualifying for top boxing PPV buys of all-time. The Oscar "Golden Boy" De La Hoya vs. Floyd "Money" Mayweather fight, nonetheless, still tops the list. And "Golden Boy" still remains boxing's all-time highest grossing PPV attraction. HBO reports list of top Pay-Per-View events in boxing's history, to wit:

1. Oscar De La Hoya vs. Floyd Mayweather, May 2007 - 2.4 million PPV buys: Mainly attributed to De La Hoya's star power, the fight was televised on HBO Pay-Per-View, with the cost to watch the fight at $55 in the U.S.

2. Mike Tyson vs. Evander Holyfield (rematch), June 1997 - 1.99 million PPV buys: 1997 Evander Holyfield-Mike Tyson heavyweight championship ear-bite rematch was still a big draw. Even a potential trilogy could still give a shot at PPV buys.

Top Pay-Per-View Boxing Events As Of May 2012

3. Mike Tyson vs. Lennox Lewis, June 2002 - 1.97 million PPV buys: The fight was shown as a joint collaboration between HBO and Showtime in the United States and on Sky Box Office in the United Kingdom. It was the highest-grossing event in pay-per-view history, generating US$106.9 million from 1.95 million buys in the USA, until it was surpassed by De La Hoya vs. Mayweather in 2007.

4. Mike Tyson vs. Holyfield (1st match), November 1996 - 1.59 million PPV buys: Tyson vs. Holyfield I, also billed as *Finally*, was a professional boxing match fought between Evander Holyfield and Mike Tyson on November 9, 1996 at the MGM Grand Garden Arena in Las Vegas, Nevada. The referee officiating the fight was Mitch Halpern. The bout was the first fight pitting the two boxers against each other and it would be followed up with a subsequent rematch.

5. Mike Tyson vs. Peter Mc Neeley, August 1995 - 1.55 million PPV buys: The fight was Tyson's first fight in 4 years, due to his prison sentence.

6. *Captured by three matches*:
  A. Oscar De La Hoya vs. Felix Trinidad, September 1999 - 1.4 million PPV buys: Trinidad reached his defining moment in the sport on Sept. 18, 1999. He got the man he had sought after for years, WBC welterweight champion Oscar De La Hoya.

  B. Evander Holyfield vs. George Foreman, April 1991 - 1.4 million PPV buys: After winning a heavyweight crown from James "Buster" Douglas, who won it with a shocking win over Tyson, Holyfield won by unanimous decision over Foreman, a 42-year-old former champion.

  C. Manny Pacquiao vs. Juan Manuel Marquez, November 12, 2011 - 1.4 PPV buys garnering much greater massive support from Latino boxing fans. The fight itself generated roughly $134.4 million dollars in domestic PPV revenue.

7. Mike Tyson vs. Frank Bruno, March 1996 - 1.37 million PPV buys: In a less anticipated rematch, Tyson regained the WBC crown stopping Bruno by a third-round knockout. Tyson won over Bruno by knockout in 1989 for the same title he lost to James Buster Douglas by knockout in round 10 in 1990.

8. Manny Pacquiao vs. Shane Mosley, May 7, 2011 - 1.3 million pay-per-view buys, generated more than $75 million in television revenue with about 700,000 buys coming via cable systems and about 600,000 coming from satellite services.

9. *Captured by three matches:*
A. Mayweather vs. Ortiz, September 17, 2011 - 1.25 million pay-per-views and $78.44 million in domestic pay-per-view revenue. The revenue generated made Mayweather-Ortiz the third-highest grossing non-heavyweight fight in history after the Pacquiao-Marquez fight. "Although the buys equaled those of Manny Pacquiao's 2008 fight with Oscar De La Hoya and virtually matched those of Pacquiao-Shane Mosley in May, Mayweather-Ortiz beat both in revenue generated because it sold for a higher price, $59.95 in standard definition and $69.95 in most markets for high definition." ESPN

B. Pacquiao vs. De la Hoya, December 6, 2008 - 1.25 million PPV buys: At the height of world economic meltdown, Oscar De La Hoya vs. Manny Pacquiao, also billed as The Dream Match, took place on December 6, 2008 at the MGM Grand Garden Arena, Las Vegas, Nevada, United States, and pulled out considerably high PPV buys. Pacquiao defeated De La Hoya via technical knockout when De La Hoya decided not to continue with the fight before the start of the ninth round.

C. Pacquiao vs. Cotto, November 14, 2009 - 1.25 million PPV buys: The said bout generated 1.25 million buys, the highest performing boxing pay-per-view event in 2009. The figure includes 650,000 buys from cable homes and 600,000 from satellite and telco homes, which includes 110,000 buys from Puerto Rico, Cotto's home state.

D. Mike Tyson vs. Razor Ruddock, June 1991 - 1.25 million PPV buys: The said event transpired as Mike Tyson's third comeback after being defeated by way of knockout in round 10 from the hands of James Buster Douglas. Razor Ruddock, who fought Mike Tyson twice, was the Canadian heavyweight champion. He was known for inventing a powerful left hook called "The Smash".

10. Holyfield vs. Lennox Lewis (1st fight), March 1999 - 1.2 million PPV buys: Lennox Lewis knocked out Donovan Ruddock and captured the top one in the World Boxing Council (WBC) rankings and eventually was declared WBC heavyweight champion. He rose to high ranks as the undisputed champion after defeating Evander Holyfield by unanimous decision in 1999.

Special Notes:

- Manny Pacquiao vs. Antonio Margarito generated 1.15 million pay-per-view buys, which created $64 million in pay-per-view revenue, on top of gate sales generated by the 41,000 in attendance.

- Manny Pacquiao vs. Joshua Clottey generated 700,000 pay per view buys and $35.3 million of pay per view revenue. The first boxing event being held at the Dallas Cowboy Stadium in Arlington, Texas.

SOURCE: HBO, Top Rank, Golden Boy, Nevada State Athletic Commission, Texas State Athletic Commission and Wikipedia.

PACQUIAO'S 'BLACK POPE' BANKING ON 'MIND-OVER-MATTER-AND-NEVER-MIND' IN EX-CATHEDRA

SEPTEMBER 1, 2010: EXCLUSIVE FROM BEVERLY HILLS, CALIFORNIA - We're in an era where absolutes are out and ambiguities in. But, for the Pacmanian think tank, truth is all in your head – and reality, a subjective extension of the brain. He advances his self-acclamation that one man's faith is another man's fairy tale, one man's beauty is another's beast, and one's sinner is another's saint. Michael Koncz, Pacquiao's resolute adviser, is probably such a one. Just call him a "Black Pope". But, unlike the Vatican Pope who claims to be infallible, Koncz is not, nor has he become a profligate.

Faith to the Best of Business

Conversely, Koncz is not bad at all. He appeals to the media: "We have to look at this fight between Manny Pacquiao and Antonio Margarito as a business." And the dignitaries, media men and their army of photographers momentarily listened carefully to every word he spoke in the elaborate ballroom of Beverly Hills Hotel.

Beauty in Its Purest Business Form

For those who think the Pacquiao-Margarito match is not worth watching at all, I suppose your thought must have gone to glorification to the feisty heads of Golden Boy Promotions. Koncz has assured that the marketing game for this November 13, 2010 event at the Dallas Cowboy Stadium in Arlington, Texas will attract most boxing fans, even the quasi ones and notwithstanding the sponsors from the giant corporations in the US.

Saint As Manny Pacquiao's Shock Absorber

Every major decision that Pacquiao has to make, Koncz may have the strongest input to it. And don't think that Pacquiao is not a great decision-maker. He is naturally a very intelligent thinker. Do not underestimate the congressman of Sarangani. It's just whatever Koncz says relative to Pacquiao consensual gesture to empower Koncz's words in ex-cathedra, that I must say, has surely entailed the blessing of the Philippine legislator. So, Koncz's sainthood is one of loyalty to Pacquiao. Mind you, Koncz is the most trusted adviser of the Maharlikan hero. Except Pacquiao or unless he does the most stupid things against the teeth of the law, no one can take away that "honorary status" from him much more that he also has become a political strategist for Team Pacquiao. And never mind, Koncz has his own game plan.

THE REAL EXCUSE: MAYWEATHER, JR HATES PACQUIAO'S RIGHT HAND - ARUM

OCTOBER 27, 2011: RAW INTERVIEW WITH HOT POTATO VIA HOLLYWOOD, CALIFORNIA - "Whatever new excuses Floyd Mayweather, Jr. has for not fighting Manny Pacquiao because of Top Rank's position in the negotiation are all bullshit!" remarks Top Rank Robert "Bob" Arum when asked about his thoughts as to why Pacquiao-Mayweather fight is not happening even after more than three years of trying to reach an agreement between the two camps. "When Floyd Mayweather, Jr. says he hates Top Rank, he really doesn't mean it," argues Arum. "What he truly hates is Manny Pacquiao's right hand."

"That's the truth!" Arum adds. "And don't get me wrong: Mayweather, Jr. knows boxing very well. He is very intelligent - too intelligent in fact, to make excuses (for not fighting Pacquiao). We are not going to chase after him. The fight is not happening all because of Mayweather, Jr. He is scared of Pacquiao's right hand; that's the real reason. He knows that Pacquiao's right hand will kill him. No matter how much money you put on the table for Mayweather, Jr., he's not going to fight Pacquiao."

For Mayweather, Pacquiao must submit to the Olympic style of random blood-testing until fight date and another one blood draw right after the fight. But, Pacquiao rejects such and, in turn, wants the same Olympic style of random blood-testing to be done 14 days before the fight and one blood test right after the fight.

Several laboratory scientists believe that with the advancement of the new medical technology and clinical research, there exists an "injectable masking agent" that potentially has the effect of powerfully concealing the therapeutic level of a drug in the blood. With this same agent, any performance enhancing drug taken for days may not surface in the laboratory analysis, according to Dr. Youngyee Hong, director of an institute for laboratory science studies. For Mayweather, Jr., the Olympic style of random-blood testing can give him the assurance that any fighter getting into a fight with him, beginning his fight with Sugar Shane Mosley on May 1 of last year and recently with Victor Ortiz, must be clean and nothing more.

"That's all I ask, nothing more!" insists Mayweather, Jr. "I'll fight Pacquiao if he submits to the Olympic style of random blood-testing until fight date and one more blood draw right after the fight."

"Also, I want the United States Anti-Doping Agency to get the blood-testing done on both of us. That's it," he adds.

Arum, conversely, rejects the idea of having the United States Anti-Doping Agency conduct the blood-testing. He otherwise believes World Anti-Doping Agency can do the best job without any bias to a foreign fighter like Pacquiao who is from the Philippines. But, both Arum and Pacquiao bluntly tell the media Mayweather, Jr. is no longer within their frame of thoughts. "Forget about Mayweather, Jr. He's no longer within our radar," says Arum.

Pacquiao, on the other hand, raises the issue about Mayweather, Jr. demanding a net due amount of $ 100,000 to perfect the contract to fight, which many promoters think is unimaginable. Both Arum and Pacquiao decline to state the reasonable amount of pay to Mayweather, Jr. in order to make the fight happen.

"I don't think there's a promoter who would agree to that proposal," says Pacquiao. "That is beyond one's imagination. He really does not want to fight. He makes new demands each time we come to terms with the previous one. It's endless. So why bother thinking about him for a fight. He is not important to me."

Mayweather, Jr. recently is open for any fight and awaits the coming days of better fights. No schedule is posted yet, as of press time. For Arum, Mayweather, Jr. is such a very fine fighter who is seen to remain undefeated until he fights Pacquiao. He believes Mayweather, Jr. is no longer relevant to boxing. "He destroys the promotional value of boxing."

Arum continues: "Now, we have guys like Timothy Bradley, Amir Khan, Sergio Martinez, Brandon Rios who are willing to fight Pacquiao. On one hand, Mayweather, Jr. is only relevant to boxing inasmuch as he wants himself to be. But boxing does not need him. And Pacquiao does not need him, either. Boxing remains alive even without Mayweather, Jr."

PACQUIAO IN THE US VERSUS PACQUIAO IN THE PHILIPPINES

*D*ECEMBER 13, 2011: HOT POTATO VIA HOLLYWOOD, CALIFORNIA - Grown in grace over the years, Pacquiao's lifetime journey is one of provocative, reflective, and thought-festive irony. Despite his claim that he has a strong faith in God, he has that side of enfeeblement which is normal in our human experience. And for sure, he is not faultless. But, that's where his strength lies. He goes to the deepest recesses of the mind. He senses the tenor of the innermost hunger of a man, a woman and a child: it's that longing to be heard. Yet, as he engages from one political sphere to another, Pacquiao changes his "color" like a chameleon distinguished by its parrot-like zygodactylous feet, in an essentially upright sense. What really changes is his weak, vacillating attempt to comprehend his susceptibility to behavior-modifying pressures by his cohorts. Tellingly, though, the moral public hopes such would not be so for long.

Whether Pacquiao adheres to the basic tenets of the biblical standard that he claims to embrace, his pathway to statesmanship is something worth-exploring. What we often do not forget about is about his hasty political endorsement. Amusing at best, he endorsed Unites States Senator Harry Reid, who faced a competitive general election for the 2010 Senate race in Nevada. Reid, indeed, engaged in a $1 million media campaign to "reintroduce himself" to Nevada's voters, which included an automated telephone voice-over device targeting the Filipino-American voters, with Pacquiao himself campaigning. Yes, Reid defeated Republican challenger Sharron Angle in the general election by the significant power of the Filipino votes.

Pacquiao, a Philippine Congressman representing Sarangani, is known for his conservative stance on the Reproductive Health Bill pending in the Philippine Congress, though his articulations were scripted by his chief of staff, Attorney Franklin Gacal, whose responsibilities are bested to lessen the burden of his congressional duties.

Despite his otherwise definitive endorsement of Reid, a pure liberal politico who advocates abortion and use of birth control substances, in the last US Senatorial Elections, Pacquiao must use his gift of discernment, if he has one. Now, the US Presidential Election is fast approaching. President Barrack Obama, a Democrat like Reid, is gearing up for his chance for a second term.

Should there be a repeat of the same kind of endorsement as with Reid, but for Obama this time? Pacquiao should continue championing the cause of the voiceless. That episode of Pacquiao's endorsement for Reid marked itself as Pacquiao's direct compromise of principles.

In the Philippines, Pacquiao has the audacity to be against artificial contraception because, he claimed, it is against the will of God. His faith leads him to strongly oppose abortion. He would fight leftwing ideologues who want to take away the right of a fetus to live. Yes, Pacquiao internalizes and empathizes with the injustices that suppress the unheard voices of the fetuses.

The same is not the belief of Reid, who advocates the right of abortion, and who professes a compromise of spiritual faith by rallying for lesbians and gays who are battling their legal recognition before the altar of matrimony.

Yes, Pacquiao and Reid truly differ in terms of principles. Pacquiao, in any way, endorsed Reid out of blind obedience to his donkey-might promoter Top Rank Godfather Robert "Bob" Arum, whose plea turned into a prayer with smoke that went to hell.

But let us forget that for now. Pacquiao is transcending and repenting. He's not static. He's dynamic. Ferreting out the truth as to where his stand should be, in the case of his utmost concern for Sarangani, is not a question of veracity, but one of foolishness. Pacquiao is an all-out deal for Sarangani, but not at the national level, where the rise of intellectualism and moral modeling is by necessity, rather than by popularity. And that's what the younger generations should expect: a willful heritage of modern Philippines and their all-time moral abiding citizenship. Notwithstanding, Pacquiao may have "a strong sense of justice and of precarious position of justice in any polity," if this writer were to borrow from one unnamed medical doctor who e-mailed Obama and to describe his faith before his rise to presidency.

Yes, Pacquiao is one of fair-minded words most of the time. But, he should not try to make sense of a common polity in the context of warring impulses, unless he is that confused. Unlike in the national political scene and in the American politics in which he immersed into and indulged with Reid, his heart for the people of Sarangani is unscripted. He sees what is at stake: the people themselves.

From the bay area up to the hinterlands of Sarangani, Pacquiao heeds the plight of the less- cared-fore and the less-informed. Never before have the natives from the far-flung sections of Sarangani seen the active faith of one from "below" who can identify with their infirmities, disenchantments, and disillusionments. Pacquiao just did what a voter expects: he projected continuously and strategically in the District he represents. In the lone district of Sarangani, Pacquiao's political ascendancy to inspire remains intact and invincible. And that's where Pacquiao should keep his graces ablaze, to retain the same model of public service for other politicians in the rest of the archipelago. No doubt, Pacquiao's heart for Sarangani is highly commendable. What he needs to fortify this is sustaining his endorsements and advocacies, reflective of his reformed, unwavering image.

BATTLING MOSLEY-PACQUAIO FOR A BETTER IMAGING RHETORIC

DECEMBER 23, 2010: CASUAL TALK FROM HOLLYWOOD, CALIFORNIA - The scheduled match between Pacquiao and Sugar Shane Mosley on May 7 at the MGM Grand Arena in Las Vegas, Nevada has been the subject of a heated debate in recent days. Armchair critics hurl insults toward Top Rank Godfather Bob Arum when he flew from Las Vegas to the Philippines last week with a "pre-destined agendum" to attend Pacquiao's 32nd birthday bash in General Santos City.

Arum may have thought that it's only proper to formally present the resolute intangible gift of a "done deal match-up" in the light of media cover-up, as alleged, for the latter's next fight. And so Golden Boy Promotions and its cohorts went on to drumbeat a suspicion that the Pacquiao-Mosley fight has been framed to happen under the dictate of Arum's economic theory of utility and standard deviation of win or loss ratio of probability. Even then, Arum has to somehow present the probable choices inclusive of their respective financial advantage to Pacquiao. And so the detractors cry out foul. To most boxing fans, "It's the better choice". To some, "It's garbage!"

Ranked second to Mayweather, Jr. in the welterweight division by Boxrec.com, Pacquiao chooses Mosley, who ranks third, to be his most formidable foe ahead of the other remaining two options: Juan Manuel Marquez and Andre Berto.

Both Pacquiao and Arum have brought a bitter divisive blow, rear-ending Golden Boy Promotions and its cohorts onto a tectonic Santa Buster. But at this stage of Pacquiao's career, even though he is still at his prime, Pacquiao has to stick to a calculated risk. The risk being that Pacquiao at 32, a Congressman representing Sarangani, Philippines, and one who aims to become President of the Philippines by the time he reaches 42, has to keep himself looking good in his upcoming last fights before he retires.

Pacquiao has to sustain his winning transformation for his political career in the Philippines, making sure that his charisma before the camera when he fights in the ring would enhance his invincibility even more, and thereby bolster his appealing image to the sentimental voting public of the Philippines. And mind you, his remaining fights to come would just be built on two factors: sustaining his legacy in the crumbling boxing world, and repackaging himself for a far better wholesome pay, and for a better imaging rhetoric. In other words, risky matches should be squashed for the sake of these two factors. From now on, Pacquiao's matches have to be "politically correct," so to speak.

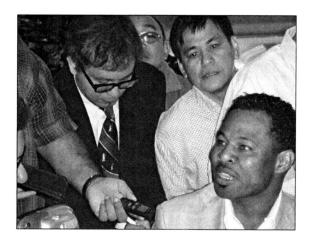

Exclusive Copyright@2012 by **PACQUIAO UNDER CROSSFIRE** *for Manny Pena; Taken at the Beverly Hills Hotel in Beverly Hills, California during Pacquiao-Mosley Press Conference in 2011.*

Of course, Mosley is a better catalyst to capture a fair household percentage of the greater Black-American market which has over 41 million heads per the 2010 US census. Aging Mosley being over-the-hill at 39 still is a good Pay-Per-View draw...but only with a Pacquiao factor. In fact, for Mosley's fight against Sergio Mora last September, fellow Yahoo! Sports writer Kevin Iole said, "Golden Boy Promotions had to be happy with the live gate (of 13,591 fans at Staples Center), though it would be a shock if the pay-per-view figures were more than 150,000."

Mosley's fight against Mayweather, Jr. generated 1.4 million buys, which suggests that he has the marketability to make a future bout with Pacquiao a mega-fight. Mosley is seemingly done. Even at his age, he is done! But for Mosley, age doesn't matter. In fact, it's like he has just won a multi-million dollar lottery jackpot. Yes, it's potentially the biggest pay of all his fights since his rise to the top of professional boxing. And that is plus a bonus chance to win over Pacquiao by knockout!

After Bob Hopkins has shown a brilliant performance against Jean Pascal that ended a majority draw, it looks like Mosley's lackluster performances both against Mayweather, Jr. and Sergio Mora have been forgotten. And so Mosley has just won big time out of that loss to Mayweather, Jr. via a unanimous decision and out of his win over Mora by a split decision, both of which give him a better margin of false hope to the less informed boxing public that he would do better than Marquez and Berto, if not knock Pacquiao out during their upcoming bout this Spring.

Yes, we might just hope aging factor would just be lost in the sub-consciousness of the boxing public. It's pathetic but that's what marketing on a calculated risk is all about. Questioning the making of the Pacquiao-Mosley fight is almost a blasphemy, at least in the mind of Arum. Whether or not such scheduled match is a prejudged choice by Arum over the prospect of having Juan Manuel Marquez or Andre Berto instead fight Pacquiao is a matter of right. So question it, and it's still Mosley-Pacquiao on May 7. Like what highly esteemed dental surgeon-turned journalist Ed de la Vega says, "Suck it up!"

TEAM PACQUIAO IN DISORDER WITH KONCZ AS THE LEAST UNDERSTOOD 'BLACK POPE'

*F*EBRUARY 2, 2011: INSIDER REPORT FROM HOLLYWOOD, CALIFORNIA - Team Pacquiao members must be on a high systolic reading as their Godfather Manny Pacquiao is scheduled to arrive here in the US to kick off his press tour with Hall of Famer Sugar Shane Mosley, who is to set foot in Beverly Hills, California. Both fighters will exchange leathers on May 7 at the MGM Grand Arena in Las Vegas, Nevada. Pacquiao will defend his World Boxing Organization Welterweight title.

There is more to address for Pacquiao than just attending the press tour. Internal issues of Team Pacquiao still linger even after years of toiling to quell the low-intensity conflicts from within. "It's like there's a cold war within the camp," says one member, speaking on condition of anonymity in an exclusive interview Tuesday at the Max's of Manila in Glendale, California. He claims he has been with Team Pacquiao since 2004. "They share the same food from the same table and also waste their ends in the same restroom but they harbor grudges and unwarranted misunderstandings [against each other]." He adds, "They fight for space to get close to Manny, except the Cebuano-speaking members who are really genuine about their goings."

Many of them, however, cannot beat the intimacy of Michael Koncz with their idol. Manny gives his full trust to this one man

Michael Koncz, but almost everyone hates this man because he has full access to Manny's financial budget, and is empowered to influence decisions as to what affairs Manny should be involved in, my source recounts to me.

"Let me tell you, others in the team are upbeat preparing to strike unscrupulous deals with their icon, only for a one-sided, underlying gain as much as they could fool," he adds.

On the other hand, Manny is reported to be getting cash advances from Top Rank as soon as he arrives in Los Angeles next week, at least 40 percent of what he will make out of his fight against Mosley. Unless otherwise directed by Koncz, the "Black Pope", Pacquiao's finances will put himself into a quagmire of far worse mismanagement. Several key players are ready to take over Koncz's de facto position in Team Pacquiao, my source warns. "They are probably worse than what they think of Michael Koncz."

My source asserts: "In March 2009, Pacquiao bought a five-bedroom, six-bath home at $2.17 million on North Plymouth Boulevard in the far edge of Melrose, technically not part of Hancock Park. Several certified brokers estimate it to cost only around $1.2 million since it was transacted during the deep housing market crash. Others say it can range between $ 1.3 and 1.5 million."

"Manny could have bought a better house than that," he laughs. Contrary to the exaggeration by Filipino news reporters, it is not even a mansion. It looks like a small apartment complex from the outside.

"I just hope Manny would one day wake up to reality," says the middle-age man, while scratching his head. "And I even doubt if Koncz can help much to control Manny's sporadic cash outflows."

"Manny," he continues, "is just too nice to everyone and I think he knows by now that many of the Team Pacquiao members are taking advantage of him."

"Koncz should lead Manny for the better," he adds.

PACQUIAO 'A WORK IN PROGRESS', LEARNING THE ARTS AND WILES - ARUM

*J*ANUARY 20, 2011: EXCLUSIVE TALK FROM BILTMORE HOTEL, LOS ANGELES, CALIFORNIA – Smarting in a signature display of his intellectual prowess and a rare distinction of optimism in his own right, celebrated Harvard lawyer Bob Arum would surely not fail his intuition, bolstering a colossal thought as a precursor for refining change. I could sense his appetite whets for more change in Emmanuel 'Manny' Pacquiao, advancing his wish in fact, and suggesting therefore that a critical transformation of his world renowned boxer into a well-rounded, tough political protégé would have brighter relevance a decade from now affecting the political landscape of the Philippines.

"Pacquiao is such an extremely intelligent person," Arum said in an exclusive interview with this writer on January 11 at the Biltmore Hotel in Los Angeles. "And he is 'a work in progress' conceivably learning the arts and wiles of politics, and I believe he is going to be very successful in what he does, and in what he will do as a politician, to the best of the Philippines."

Pacquiao, 32, is the incumbent congressman of the lone district of Sarangani, Philippines. He has been rumored to be aspiring to capture the top post of the Maharlikan nation some years from now. Arum, 80, said nevertheless; that he is banking and will be supporting one-hundred percent on Pacquiao's foray to become president of the Philippines.

"Having the lineage (of Jew) to live longer than a hundred years, I believe that will happen in my lifetime, and I would humbly take that as my joy for the Philippines," Arum said. "I tell you, Pacquiao will become President of the Philippines when he reaches 42," Arum added.

Figures compiled by the Office for U.S. Bureau of National Statistics suggest that there are nearly three times as many Jewish people who are 100 or older than there are in the general population. In the 2001 Census, twice the number of those in the Jewish community were 90 or more, the *Jewish Chronicle Online* reports.

Arum has set his eyes on a plan to highlight Washington as one of the listed states for the media tour of the Pacquiao-Mosley fight on May 7 at the MGM Grand Arena in Las Vegas, Nevada. And there's more to it than just promoting this upcoming fight. Arum has asked his close friend, Majority Senate Leader Harry Reid, to arrange a meeting between President Barrack Obama and Pacquiao to discuss the 'possibility of annexing the Philippines' to the US, Arum joked and laughed heartily.

Arum has asked Senator Reid to fix a courtesy visit with President Obama at the White House while Pacquiao will be on a media tour in Washington this early spring. Arum has no word of confirmation for such meeting as of this writing.

Senator Reid won his fifth term as Senator, whom Pacquiao endorsed, and is bent to give Pacquiao the favor of making possible the meeting with Obama. In addition to Pacquiao's endorsement, the statistical report from *Las Vegas Sun* said that Hispanic voters proved key to Reid's victory. Reid is the senior United States Senator from Nevada, serving since 1987. A member of the Democratic Party, he has been the Senate Majority Leader since January 2007, having previously served as Minority Leader and Minority and Majority Whip, his public record states.

As for Pacquiao's progression in the sphere for increasing public approval in the Philippines, would these American brains – Obama, Reid, and Arum – in return become synergistically the catalysts of Pacquiao's transformation to the top post? I rather suppose there must be a greater force than these three.

OBAMA-PACQUIAO MEETING A CHANCE OF DIPLOMACY, NOT MENDICANCY

*F*EBRUARY 8, 2011: SIDE BAR COMMENTARY FROM HOLLYWOOD, CALIFORNIA – I rather find it a bit of a fascination and an honor to touch on this specific topic about the purported "meeting" between boxer-turned-actor Sarangani Congressman Emmanuel "Manny" Pacquiao and US President Barack Obama.

This meeting is a matter of "arrangement" by Senate Majority Leader Harry Reid, whom Pacquiao endorsed in the last US senatorial elections, which some journalists in the Philippines gave so much hype about, as if it is too close from happening anytime, as a "side-trip" consequent to the unconfirmed Washington press conference, as of this writing, for the Mosley-Pacquiao fight on May 7 at the MGM Grand Arena in Las Vegas, Nevada.

In my exclusive conversation with Top Rank Godfather Robert "Bob" Arum last January 11 at the Biltmore Hotel in Los Angeles, he said such a potential meeting would be a non-official chance of diplomacy. Therefore, it should not be taken as an "official chance for mendicancy", in the theorist's delicate parlance.

Another, I must say that such possible meeting can only be "official" if the 15th Congress of the Philippines would so empower Pacquiao to act as a spokesperson, only for purposes of capturing the best of his moment with Obama. And I don't think Obama would not love to capture the limelight of such a moment. He would rather embrace the magnitude of that meeting in his capacity as President of the United States of America, so that he might reciprocate something better for the Republic of the Philippines, if not for Pacquiao alone.

But here's the smile-inducer for Pacquiao's fans and for those who want to be a part of the entourage of Team Pacquiao to the White House: Obama had said he will have plenty of time to campaign for reelection in 2012. If Obama really wanted to be more expansive of his campaign down to the rising grassroots of Filipino-Americans who constitute the second largest group of Asians in the US, then his fledgling campaign team should waste no time.

As reported in the *Los Angeles Times* on February 6, 2011, Obama's campaign manager Jim Messina "spent last week hop-scotching across the country to hold sessions with prominent donors in San Francisco, Los Angeles, New York and Boston. . .His outreach is a part of an intense push to rebuild the finance operation that helped Obama raise a record $ 745 million in 2008."

Now I don't think Obama would dare solicit some dollars from Pacquiao out of this "chance-meeting", however unofficial it may be. Oh yes, for Obama, he cannot do so from a foreigner. The teeth of US law are too sharp for that type of transaction. He would lecture one on that issue.

Neither should Pacquiao solicit some dollars for his hospital project in Sarangani, solely to boost his performance rating, being a duly-elected Congressman of Sarangani, and for the fulfillment of his campaign promise in the last congressional elections of the Philippines. Pacquiao should have a clear grasp of what it takes to be an official representative of the Philippines. Should the Philippine Congress so empower Pacquiao to act on such "meeting" as the official one or as a matter of "spur-of-the-moment" as the "Ambassador-of-Goodwill-in-fact", so to speak, then why not? For a meeting to be called "official", both public offices of the respective countries they represent should mark their respective book of records as the "Obama-Pacquiao meeting", or some sort.

I suppose that "chance-meeting" would just be a campaign-booster for both Obama and Pacquiao. I mean, a personal appointment, at least according to my understanding of Arum's statement.

Of course, for Pacquiao, it's for his fight, country and for the lone district of Sarangani he represents, and sure, for the betterment of his public image as he leads himself to the prospect of joining the presidential derby at least a decade from now. And for Obama, it's all about solidifying his appeal to the Filipino-American voting populace.

THE ZEN OF EMMANUEL D. PACQUIAO: BOXER, ENTERTAINER, ACTOR, BUILDER OF FAITH

NOVEMBER 10, 2010: HOLLYWOOD, CALIFORNIA — After his brilliant performance last Saturday at the Dallas Cowboy Stadium claiming a record eighth world weight-class title by annihilating Antonio Margarito via unanimous decision, Pacquiao keeps his composure nearly untouched by the pressures he gets from being one of the top personalities of the world.

It seems that he senses what his victory and inspiration would bring to his Maharlikan nation and for the healing to the less-inspired, regardless of social disparity and racial identity. Pacquiao has become a world icon of all time, so to speak, in the sport of boxing, and inevitably beyond.

In the days before his scheduled fight against Margarito, and as he jogged in the hills of Hollywood, he knew for sure what he had lost and gained out there, more than 8,000 miles away, deep in the hinterlands of the third world country, out there along the streets of General Santos City more than 15 years ago, and there before in his formative years.

Pacquiao drifted to losing the pride of oneself from the devastating evils of poverty and at the same time, lifted his spirit by gaining the faith that he would forever treasure, particularly from his wakefulness when he heard that "super-natural voice" inspiring his desire to please boxing fans around the world and to give honor to his countrymen.

Through the holes of the rooftop of his family's "nipa hut" that offered segments of views of the starry skies of that rebel-infested region of Mindanao, if not just drops of blood upon the miasma in the rainforest or quite expectedly drops of rain when the weather seemed either kind or unkind, and from the sighs at dawn of his mother, Dionisia, who somehow cared less but for the survival of her family from the bondage of almost nothingness, Pacquiao's inimitable persona would be enough to crack open the formidable collision between moralistic stupidity and fearless regard to each moment he envisioned.

Less forgotten for the moment was not only the long history of how the estimated 92 million people of the Philippines, the world's 12th most populous country, became jubilant each time he won a fight in recent years, notwithstanding the more inspired additional 11 million Filipinos who live outside the Philippines. They must have watched Pacquiao stories all unfolding before them, and read more stories about him as though he were once their close friend, as though he were still in the personal "life-movie" that his life has become.

Pacquiao completed his elementary education at Saavedra Saway Elementary School in General Santos City, but dropped out of high school due to extreme poverty. Then, he left his home at age fourteen because his mother, who had six children, was not making enough money to support her family. It was then that Manny Pacquiao had to engage the dehumanizing aspects of boxing. In the ring, he was feisty as ever, gutsy, and combative with an enterprising fire, and a spirit of sportsmanship, and religious fortitude.

"Manny is really tough, and has no fear, and he works so hard, even in his young years," said Mang Ben who was Pacquiao's first boxing trainer. "And he is a very religious kid. He always gives offering to the nuns somewhere in Manila even if he fails to win a fight."

When this writer met Pacquiao here in Los Angeles before his fight against Lehlohonolo Ledwaba of Africa on June 23, 2001, the same personality was bedecked in a rugged sweat shirt and blue jeans – which he does up to this date, bringing to light such rare humility.

Pex Aves, a noted political crusader and commentator during the era of former President Ferdinand E. Marcos, knew there was more to Pacquiao than just the bruises the latter got from his opponents' punches and jabs. "He is a very religious fighter. He hits his opponents in the ring a murderous shot, and then says, 'This is nothing personal. It's just my job to fight for a living,'" said Aves, who used to pick up Pacquiao at the Los Angeles International Airport each time Pacquiao came to prepare for a potential fight arrangement in the US.

Almost a decade since then, Pacquiao by far exhibits the same character: A fighter who never leaves his enemy without extending mercy and grace – an act of class rarely seen among athletes in blood sport. Twice in the same manner when he fought Margarito in the tenth, eleventh and in the twelfth, Pacquiao cautiously confined himself to slow down and more careful not to viciously inflict more injuries to the end and even asked the Referree Laurence Cole to check on his foe's right lower orbital damage.

Even in the desolation of Erik Morales, David Diaz, Miguel Cotto, Oscar De La Hoya, Ricky Hatton, Jorge Solis, the same heart took time to demonstrate the spirit of mercy and grace. Yes, even in the early days of his professional boxing career, the same was shown when he first knocked Dele Decierto out in round 2 of his fourth professional fight on record in Mandaluyong, Metro Manila in 1995.

Pacquiao felt less the pressures that potentially go with winning and losing. For him, it's up to the higher power. Never forgotten was his performance as life, and life as performance, both public and private. He may have more winnings and losing outside of the ring of madness. Whenever he was hurt from boxing, he confided to nobody, not even to painkiller pills, but to the Most High.

Being a daredevil fighter, he enjoyed expanding his contacts even to the point of engulfing himself in the unknown world of the scoundrels, sycophants and some numbskull politicians, loving the glazed feeling when he hardly knew where such would lead him, even to the moment of submitting his power of choice to someone's terms in full trust and confidence but less for himself unknowingly at times, which most dishonest would hunt such opportunity.

Meanwhile, a terrible pulling and hauling and an awful straining is happening beneath the artifice of Pacquiao all remarkably inspiring him to become a presidential candidate in the Philippines twelve years from now, as of this writing. All this presumptive pushing could function within the context of popularity and pure fame. Will the Filipinos be prepared to work out together with Pacquiao beyond the consuming crisis of their lives?

PACQUIAO: THE GODFATHER

*D*ECEMBER 10, 2010 – Love him or hate him! That's what he likes! Not that this would help him in landing a role that will revitalize his prematurely flagging career in movie-making in the Philippines, nor does it have any implication of his political influence in the Maharlikan nation for his birthday celebration on December 17 in General Santos City, Philippines.

Emmanuel "Pacman" D. Pacquiao, greatly respected among international critics and the public world, will turn thirty-two and would be a kind of attraction on his birthday bash. And keen observers, celebrities from showbizlandia and his nuclear family and all may somehow have a glimpse of his linking image on that day. "The Godfather", a 1972 American gangster-drama film which received Academy Awards for Best Picture, Best Actor, and Best Adapted Screenplay, has been chosen by Maria Geraldine "Jinkee" Jamora-Pacquiao to be the theme of her husband's birth anniversary.

"The Godfather" story, spanning ten years from 1945 to 1955 and chronicling the fictional Italian American Corleone crime family which debuted in silver screen before Pacman was born. Part I came out in 1972, The Godfather Part II was released in 1974, and The Godfather Part III in 1990. This is said to be Pacman's favorite American film. It is a story characterized by murder, drugs, corruption and betrayal within the family and society as a whole.

Conversely, Pacman, a Sarangani lawmaker and a potential peace negotiator under the current Aquino administration for the resolution of the more than four decades of chronic and sporadic high intensity conflict with the New People's Army and the Muslim rebels in the Philippines, would like to portray himself in the best of Al Pacino, the leading figure of that film, both in attire and dramatic acts. Prompting the Pacmanian culture, there will also be visitors and guests who will wear 'The Godfather-look' outfit. But, is this really a fitting theme or image for the golden-hearted, godly icon of the Philippines?

PACQUIAO-POPE BENEDICT XVI MEETING CAN HAPPEN ANYTIME - ARUM

*J*ULY 6, 2011: HOT POTATO EXCLUSIVE - In an exclusive interview Tuesday at Fortune Gym on Sunset Boulevard in Hollywood, celebrated Harvard lawyer Robert "Bob" Arum, who was instrumental along with US Senator Harry Reid in making the Obama-Pacquiao meeting at the White House a reality early this year, sees relevance for Philippine icon and Congressman Emmanuel Pacquiao to meet the Holy See.

"I knew the Holy See has to be very pleased with Pacquiao's stance on birth control and his opposition to passing out condoms," says Arum referring to Pacquiao's opposition to the Reproductive Health Bill in the Philippines which has been regarded to "set the stage for other anti-life laws or so-called D.E.A.T.H. bills (acronym for death, euthanasia, abortion, two-child policy, and homosexuality)." The said proposed Bill is principally authored by Congressman Edcel C. Lagman of Albay.

As a devout Catholic, Pacquiao campaigns for natural family planning methods, particularly abstinence. This is consistent with the stance of the Catholic faith through which Pope Benedict XVI seeks to become the moral authority of the world. In other words, the Vatican is demanding a role in regulating world politics and economy based on its Christian ethics and that's where Pacquiao's task as a lawmaker fills the role of advocacy on social conscience and responsibility.

Arum stresses: "The question is timing; There is no question that if Pacquiao has the time, we could arrange a meeting for him with the Pope. And I'm sure the Archbishop of Manila could do the same thing." Meanwhile, in another exclusive with a Pacquiao confidant who is an active cantor of the Roman Catholic Church, Helena Buscema says the Filipino icon is eager to visit the Pope at the Vatican. And in fact, Buscema also notes that an arrangement can easily be done any time with her current contacts in the Vatican.

Most top figures of the United States, like the presidents, and other key dignitaries of the world, traditionally regard a meeting with the Pope a significant milestone and also an ultimate and a formidable political empowerment of one's authority. Based on the prophetic intelligence briefings of the Vatican, the Pope is calling for the globalization of politics. A meeting with Pacquiao might just push this agenda even further.

PACQUIAO BECOMING THE "SAMSON OF OLD"?

NOVEMBER 9, 2011: HOT POTATO VIA LAS VEGAS, NEVADA – You really don't have to be a boxer, a boxing writer or a boxing judge to be a critical observer of boxing. Any observer will know Pacquiao's advantage over Marquez. Sure, it would help to know them both, critically observe their fights, styles and vital statistics and other relevant or somehow pertinent factors. But the key is all about discernment over mere reliance on the knowledge of the principles of that said ring of madness. In fact, a layman's thinking may at times come right to the point and, for sure, better than so called "boxing experts."

Pacquiao vs. Marquez III brings to mind several points of interest, considering the intense rivalry Pacquiao and Marquez (nay not just between them but Philippines vs. Mexico), have had spanning about a decade, perhaps more, and since the time of the great Flash Elorde in the world of boxing.

I personally do not discount the element of surprise that Marquez can bring against Pacquiao. But, Marquez is running 39, trying to defy his physiological limits in terms of quicker reflex and better resistance than the younger Pacquiao who is only turning 33 this December. Remember: Pacquiao was not in his prime when he first fought Marquez in 2004 which was scored a draw, however controversial it has become. And Marquez was already on the decline when he lost to Pacquiao in 2008 via a split decision.

During both encounters, Pacquiao was just a one-dimensional fighter, solely relying on his lightning left and had predictable footwork. Now, Pacquiao has surged to a higher level with his new killer-right and unpredictable footwork and amazing hand speed, perhaps much higher and mightier than anyone would know.

While Marquez is a talented fighter, Pacquiao is not just that. Yes, Pacquiao is a gifted fighter whose power, intelligence and faith he did not create nor earn. All these are gifts from above, given to him as unmerited favor. But these same gifts can pass away. History is replete with historical figures that fell from glory because of mismanagement of the gifts they had received. King David, King Solomon, King Nebuchadnezzar, Moses and more. So long as he keeps up his faith, Pacquiao won't be like one of them and especially like Samson of the Scripture who was once gifted with power.

"Yet even though Samson grew up with a great gift from God, he lacked integrity. He had charisma without character. Samson was a walking contradiction. He could perform the greatest feats of strength through the power of the Holy Spirit immediately after he spent the night in the house of a prostitute" (Judges 16:1-3).

Unlike Pacquiao, Samson never showed any concern for God nor for his nation, Israel. His acts were self-centered — he protected his own interests. He was a loner who loved loose women from the enemy camp. He used God more than he allowed God to use him.

Samson did great damage to the Philistines but mostly for his own ego and personal fulfillment. Had he been a vessel more obedient to God, the Philistines might have been driven out or even destroyed. There may have never been a Goliath or a Philistine army for David and Israel to fight. Samson did not destroy the Philistines; he only bothered and hindered them. Samson truly fulfilled the angel's words: ". . .he shall *begin* to deliver Israel out of the hand of the Philistines" (Judges 13:5).

But, is Pacquiao becoming Samson of Old? Definitely no! We hope he never will.

History is filled with men of power just like Samson. Behind the facade of the man of God we have sometimes found an adulterer, drug addict, drunkard or homosexual. We often wonder how men who preach with great anointing and perform miracles can have lifestyles filled with sin. "How could this be?" we wonder. Look at Samson!

Unlike Pacquiao, Samson mistook grace for tolerance. He thought God would keep overlooking his sins and his rotten attitude. But Samson eventually found out what all transgressors discover: "Your sins will find you out." There is a payday. The seeds which have been sown will produce a crop. Samson died blind and in fetters. His full potential was never realized.

The ancient inspiration tells us in Romans 11:29, "God's gifts and His call are irrevocable—He never withdraws them when once they are given, and He does not change His mind about those to whom He gives His grace or to whom He sends His call" (AMP).

God does not withdraw His gifts, yet the life of Samson shows us we cannot sin behind the scenes and think we will not be caught. We can only abuse them and lose their operative power. Solomon told us we cannot walk on hot coals and expect our feet not to get burned (Proverbs 6:28). Sin leaves its mark and God will see to it that un-confessed sin eventually comes into the open. Gifted ones today need to learn Samson's lesson early to avoid his fate, and to keep their power from going sour.

Just because one prays in public and reads his Bible does not mean he is connected to God but just may be to his own "god." Matthew 7:21-24 is clear on this, saying : "Not everyone who says to Me, 'Lord, Lord,' will enter the kingdom of heaven; but he who does the will of My Father who is in heaven. Many will say to Me on that day, 'Lord, Lord, did we not prophesy in Your name, and in Your name cast out demons, and in Your name perform many miracles?' And then I will declare to them, 'I never knew you; depart from Me, you who practice lawlessness.'"

And we resort to saying: "We are just humans. We make mistakes." That's pure B.S.! Just because we are justified by faith, we rationalize that we somehow have the "license" to commit intentionally immoral acts. Sanctification is not a one-time event. It's a process. And it is to last a lifetime for better Christian experience.

BOWEL MOVEMENT WITH LIVE WORMS OVER PACQUIAO'S CHOICE AS HIS NEXT OPPONENT

JANUARY 4, 2012 – Pacquiao may need to get back to the basics. I'd actually call this issue bullshit if I didn't feel its relevance were less insulting. I haven't actually told people how to make a hydrogen bomb out of baking soda in their garages. It's even less academic. But, what does it mean when one dreams about having a bowel movement with live worms?

Well, dreaming of a bowel movement with live worms means that "one is successfully getting rid of his old habits, ways and thinking patterns" that are corrupting his self. Which in this case comes to mind about Pacquiao's likelihood to put excuses first over what's of top priority.

While I continue to break down the components of the surrounding circumstances he is facing relative to his journey from boxing to showbiz and then to politics and vice versa, I still believe Pacquiao would have to stand firm and exercise his power of choice. That, I would truly admire. But certainly it does apply to his likely choice to abandon a treacherous road that would lead him to face the top two brilliant counter-punchers we have today: Juan Manuel Marquez and Floyd Mayweather, Jr.

Consider this absolute sequence: 2012's two blockbuster matches would logically highlight fights of Pacquiao and Marquez first on their fourth encounter, then Pacquiao and Mayweather, Jr.

That's it! For Arum, even if Mayweather, Jr.'s scheduled commencement of his 90-day jail term this Friday, January 6, would not take place, Marquez is still the logical choice.

No need to discuss about Balaam and his talking donkey. For a brilliant Jew like Arum, Balaam and his donkey stand in infamy as the paragon of apostasy. No need to purge the donkey either. In fact, Arum has something big to correct. Pacquiao's recent highly controversial victory over Marquez under the judges' scorecards did not translate a better image to Top Rank's credibility and likeability. It may have damaging effects upon Pacquiao's campaign to increase value-added winability to product endorsements. His attempted deals to penetrate deeper into segmenting the American market have fallen short.

In sad contrast, Pacquiao is becoming less than a diamond, becoming so defensive of his "victory" over Marquez. Less tellingly, he has somehow lost that winning aura to appealing the mainstream American product promoters. I doubt if he would have a better endorsement than what he had contracted with Nike and Hewlett-Packard, however less the dollars he was paid out of those deals compared to the American celebrities' power-edge.

Inside reports have it he's failing his endorsements with less expected returns. This, Top Rank, which has the signatory power to package Pacquiao's image-building relative to product endorsement in the US, must now define better strategies to repackage its protégé's prematurely declining marketability. Pacquiao's "darling image" has been diminishing before the wide range of America's boxing fans inclusive of the quasi ones, especially before the high-powered camera. His image back in the Philippines as well is becoming like a fish that slowly rots from the head, nothing less.

His fan base is dissipating also because of some controversies he had outside of the ring. Everything adds up and in fact, the same controversies yield a multiplier effect in that he may need to make a quick visit to the Pope of Rome for remission, so to speak. And Arum, in his earnest mind of more than 200 IQ reverence, knows what's at stake for Pacquiao.

The Pacquiao politics by far is shorthand for Arum's simpler admiration of what life should be. Arum knows Pacquiao's critical pathway to greatness. He is the sole architect of Pacquiao's rise to greater height to this day. Pacquiao's image may have just become Arum's masterpiece. It's all about the IQ over those worms with bowel movement in a dream; those habit-forming excuses, denials and less than genuine heart spell for the Philippine flag. It's all about what matters most all for the true hardcore boxing fans and the paying boxing public. It should be all about the real "Pacquiao" over sycophants, enchanters and less informed fans. And it's rather all about facing the real challenge in 2012.

Pacquiao vs. Marquez would just be right, as a matter of urgency, before getting the much harder, sleeker counter-puncher Mayweather, Jr. at sight. Or, Pacquiao and Arum would just leave an indelible bad mark in the history of boxing.

$ 300 - 500 MILLION UPSWING RETURN FOR PACQUIAO-MAYWEATHER FIGHT

JANUARY 24, 2012: EXCLUSIVE, HOLLYWOOD, CALIFORNIA – Mayweather, Jr. vs. Pacquiao remains the most hotly anticipated battle on earth, as of this early 21st century. The unstopping beats they both spell around keep amplifying-despite Mayweather, Jr.'s current short-term jail sentence to begin on June 1, plus community service primary to domestic violence and least of Pacquiao's complex political affairs. Potential investors from the multi-billionaires circle never stop coming up with numbers bearing an up-swing likely return between $ 300-500 million, an inside report apart from Top Rank reveals.

Consider this: selling at $89.99 for Pay-Per-View with an estimated 3.5 million viewers, Pacquiao-Mayweather fight can generate over $ 300 million, not including sponsors, live gate ticket sales and merchandise. With an extensive six-month marketing and advertising campaign, the Mayweather, Jr. vs. Pacquiao boxing event can easily surpass the De la Hoya-Mayweather fight which generated 2.4 million pay-per-view buys. Forecasting the vastness of its potential and commercial network of exposures, Las Vegas is definitely a better choice than having the fight held at the ready-made site, Dallas Cowboy Stadium in Texas, the report adds.

Knowing the unsurpassed pay-per-view figures of the Mayweather-De la Hoya fight, a quick check of Pacquiao's vital performance for now could just suffice to set the tone of optimism. Pacquiao's promoter Top Rank Godfather Robert Arum's drive to have the Pacquiao-Mayweather fight be held in Las Vegas might just be right considering the several interests of big time investors hovering over the perfection of the contract between Pacquiao and Mayweather.

Arum was dismayed by what took place in Texas during the Pacquiao-Clottey fight on March 13, 2010. The same fight was rewarded with a paid crowd of 36,371 and a gate of only $6,359,985, according to post-fight tax reports filed with Texas boxing regulators. The report counted the complimentary tickets delivered to sponsors, media outlets and others. In fact, it attracted 41,843, well short of the 50,994 that was previously announced, but still an epic number for boxing, according to reports. And the bout only drew 700,000 pay-per-view buys and earned $35.3 million in domestic revenue. On the other hand, Pacquiao-Margarito fight generated 1.15 million pay-per-view buys and $64 million in pay-per-view revenue, according to HBO.

Back to Las Vegas, the Pacquiao-Mosley fight generated over 1.3 million pay-per-view buys versus the Pacquiao-Cotto fight which generated 1.25 million buys and $70 million in domestic pay-per-view revenue, making it the most watched boxing event of 2009, according to report. Likewise, Pacquiao-De la Hoya fight generated 1.25 million pay-per-view buys.

But the Pacquiao-Mayweather fight is a different case. Both fighters are phenomenal. They are the top two fighters in the world today, both with compelling charisma. With about three years of on-and-off frenzy of media and fans about it, they both ride the tide of best exposure of all. In schizophrenic swings, even quasi-boxing fans' interest grows larger and much more contagious and earnest to talk about it and debate about it with each passing day: Pacquiao-Mayweather's potential fight has become resident of the larger boxing public's sub-consciousness.

Never forget: Pacquiao is reaching his target market in a wider range, even at a grander scale, as manifested on the front cover of major magazines and other mainstream media, such as Time and Sports Illustrated and his several appearances in hot TV shows in the U.S., breaking the walls of cultural and racial indifference. He's been consistent of his pay-per-view sales production that hits 1.4 million from his recent fight with Juan Manuel Marquez. And it's true; Pacquiao has his genuine fans in every ethnic group, symbolic of a phenomenal metamorphosis of his international appeal to this racially divided American public.

But, as for Mayweather, one really does not need legal jargon to win an argument. He is a marketing genius in his own right and he can very well determine whether he captures the hearts of his American community in general and even the quasi ones. Being still widely popular beyond boxing even at the lower middle-age bracket which constitutes the wider paying audience of sports and entertainment, he is still well-loved as "Pretty Boy" by the Black American community with aggregate spending power of over $ 900 billion, according to 2010 US States Bureau of Census' statistical survey, plus the much wider segments of the American sports enthusiasts and quasi ones. He by far identifies with the ever wild minds of the young generations who care nothing but having fun and living a life to its fullest. The same bracket heightens his likeability and fondness, boasting his less marginal, sweeping promotional appeal through mass media.

Meanwhile, "Pacquiao" has become a household name among the Filipino-Americans and even among the Mexican-Americans and more. The fact that Pacquiao has penetrated the American market even unto the halls of Hollywood celebrities makes him equally phenomenal with Mayweather's massive appeal, banking the Filipino-Americans' solid $89 billion spending power.

Yes, with Mayweather's flawless professional record of forty-two fights, he is by far seen as the reigning "controversial boxing" hero in the Black American community which has an explosive population of over 42 million in the U.S. based on the United States Bureau of Census' statistical survey in 2010. His affinity with the general American public is one of promising appeal.

Sure, the immortality of boxing from the sundown of each Saturday would just be as alive as these two fighters would finally stage their battle not later than 2012. While Pacquiao mounts aggression both in the media and in the courts of law in view of the defamation lawsuit on steroid allegation, Mayweather, Jr. projects a less offensive but tactical play only to slide and evade from the harsh measures of the law.

However, both Pacquiao and Mayweather, Jr. might just amicably resolve the prolonged court battle. At this juncture, the same fighters may have nearly the same fearless might even at their near-retiring stage.

PACQUIAO'S PRIVACY UNDER SCRUTINY

*F*EBRUARY 28, 2012 – Philippines' GMA sports newscaster Manolo Chino Trinidad puts it right: "Before Tim Tebow and Jeremy Lin, there was Manny Pacquiao who, without fail, prayed before and after each fight. . ." Nothing is really new to Pacquiao's classic act in the ring of madness. At least, that's what he has enthralled the worldwide television audience each time he kneels in the corner and lights up the flame of prayer in his heart to open and, consequently, to close his every ring performance.

Like us, he surely is not alone. His life is an open book to the entire universe with all the heavenly intelligences investigating his affairs and doing their respective ministerial tasks and manifesting guidance in unbelievable ways.

What the human agents and other investigative journalists would do as they delve into Pacquiao's unwarranted entries affecting his moral standing would be nothing compared to the transparency that these celestial agents have been privileged to investigate.

What's most comforting is Pacquiao's public witnessing as he studies with his family and friends the Scripture. And the effect is being felt, indeed. What Helena Buscema, voice tutor of Pacquiao and charismatic congregational song and praise leader at the Christ the King Catholic Church here in Hollywood, shared to this writer, is one moment of awakening.

"His face lights up when I mentioned to him about a specific passage of the Scripture," says Buscema during the Pacquiao-Bradley Press Conference in the famous celestial-themed Crystal Ballroom of Beverly Hills Hotel in Beverly Hills last February 21. "It's like he has so much peace in his heart. Really, I am seeing a different Pacquiao." Buscema, out of her utmost regard and jubilance, brought a devotional bible. She said she will give it to Pacquiao.

While it is true that using God's name to justify an outward appeal to one's own family is undesirable, it might just be too premature to discredit his manifested change at this time. Many, though, will see it as an effort to regain trust out of optimism amidst the numerous controversies and to rectify his popularity which is deemed as plummeting.

But Pacquiao is transforming – we're talking conversion and metamorphosis – and perfecting his ways is the business of the Holy Spirit. Conversely, he is just as perfect at this stage of his engagement with Jesus Christ, his Creator, Lord and Savior.

With his moment by moment relationship with the Most High as he has told, no one should be surprised if Pacquiao goes to the forefront and publicly admits what he so publicly denies. It's all between Pacquiao and his God, if indeed He is his God, who knows the deepest recesses of his mind. Tellingly, true repentance only comes after true confession. Though they both are gifts, they are inseparable. Whether or not Pacquiao is truly intent on submitting to this sanctifying process, his case only rests seriously with an investigative judgment before the entire universe.

Could this be Pacquiao's "inconvenient truth" for feeling that he is being watched all the time? Even then, there's only one boxer who has truly inspired the Filipinos, inclusive of the less cared, the disenchanted and the disillusioned, if so indeed they, collectively, are not deceived. And Pacquiao couldn't just be scrutinized as much as he believes. Above all else, a higher authority exists. Pacquiao knows.

PACQUIAO THE ENLIGHTENED AND ANOINTED ONE

APRIL 26, 2012: HOT POTATO – Pacquiao insists: "I will not stay long in boxing because 'He' (God) said: 'You have done enough. You have made yourself famous but this is harmful.'"

Let's extrapolate and break down the first clause of the last statement: "You have made yourself famous. . ." I wonder if this contradicts God's statement in Jeremiah 1:18, stating, "Today I have made you like a fortified city, an iron pillar, and a bronze wall." Notice Pacquiao's quote is Pacquiao-centered: YOU HAVE made YOURSELF famous. . .and Scripture's quote is God-centered: "I HAVE made you like a fortified city. . ." In other words, it's all about the issue of authorship.

Now, Pacquiao's claim sows seeds of disillusionment and disenchantment. Is it really Pacquiao who made himself famous? Was it really the voice of "God", our Creator, Lord and Savior, in the name of Jesus Christ, in his dream?

Several psychics in Los Angeles, especially in the sections surrounding Palazzo where Pacquiao and his cohorts stay in the last phase of every training for a boxing match, claim they have experienced a similar event.

In fact, two of them told this author long ago that God talks to them directly, even as they read their bibles and offer lighted candles and burn incense before these man-made statues, to which Pacquiao fixes his eyes upon. And they quote passages of Scripture in the manner more sincere, more spontaneous and even more humbling than Pacquiao's bubbling spirit. Few would discount if Pacquiao had the same flash in his dream of the kind of metaphysical engagement. Many would not discount either if he had really such a heavenly- inspired encounter in his dream, not to blaspheme God's name. Many have been skeptical about Pacquiao's revelation as his articulations and actuations get tested with the Scripture he claims to uphold.

Nevertheless, the same is said to be Pacquiao's recent revelation during an interview with DZMM, a radio station in the Philippines, in which he claims he was visited by "God" in a dream and asked him to retire from boxing. Nothing is new, really, as Pacquiao, 33, has been contemplating retiring from boxing several times before, most especially now that his popularity is plummeting within the confines of the Filipino populace.

But, Pacquiao may have just espoused awakening issues which have historical antecedents, according to some of his associates. These same associates have become a bit apprehensive that Pacquiao may have gone overboard: popularizing the sweeping change of his private behavior relative to his newfound faith. In many respects, Pacquiao's story is lamentable. His star rose and shone but a few dazzling moments before plunging into pantheistic darkness prior to this late development.

Sure, no one should dwell on Pacquiao's aberrations with pleasure. But, on biblical perspective, they hold special lessons for our time. To many, Pacquiao's just fairly a smiling and charming icon but not an incredibly intelligent creature, contrary to top-speed Illuminati's expectations. Many have whispered about it in the deep circle of the US media. In the national political arena of the Philippines, he is in deep crisis. Although it somewhat has subsided after his confession of faith, questions about his sincerity and less than humble acts have flared repeatedly. Numerous efforts have been made by his camp to dampen the surrounding issues lately. But, each new attempt has only added more fuel to the fire.

One insider says: "It would be difficult to invent a new hearsay but we think he's a changed man...But, we do not know if his new character will prove to last – Michael Koncz, his dark angel, still gets on top of him."

No doubt, Pacquiao's overly broadcasted bible studies may have undercut his intent, hoping that such outward manifestation would translate into political votes. The same may have just agitated the awakening minds of the Filipinos who have now seen his antics; especially that he has become so obsessed with his desire for higher and loftier political goals in the country.

Pacquiao knows how ridiculous he has become being now too close to becoming "Saint Manny Pacquiao". The Catholic Church must be on the verge of committing the most grievous decision it ever conceived in the annals of its history. If Pacquiao is intent on using God's word to advance his self-subscribed political agenda, then let him be anathema.

Pacquiao's association with the donkeys here in the US speaks of it all. His unofficial visit to the White House to meet US President Barrack Hussein Obama early last year and his endorsement of US Senator Harry Reid in the last senatorial elections both mark a distinct view of his being lacking in surety of conservative principles.

Think of this and make no mistake that as the US presidential election is fast approaching in the fall, Pacquiao would dampen his might and endorse a candidate from the Democratic Party whose beliefs are not consistent with the biblical principles "he now judiciously upholds" such as advocacies for gays and lesbians right to marry the same sex, rights to abortion (killing fetuses) and other non-liberating issues contrary and not foundational to his newfound faith. That's how gullible Pacquiao is with external powers.

Meanwhile, new entrants to his circle particularly develop new waves of fanaticism. He memorizes biblical texts and summons his sycophants in the media to make them public after days of rehearsing, even amidst of his lack of in-depth understanding of the implications of the principles of interpretations. His articulations have become so predictable just as the scripts he reads in some seeming interplays of exclusive interviews in front of the cameras. For him, it's the only way to rectify his unrighteous acts in private and make them boldly righteous enough in public.

Though he has become the historic saving grace of the Arroyo administration, Pacquiao has now met so much skepticism about his self-serving political agenda, to the point of adulterating his spirituality.

And the hardest thing about Pacquiao being a headline celebrity is that he has become the brilliant product of Top Rank Godfather Robert "Bob" Arum's ingenuity, even to the best of his one wish: To see the Filipino superstar become the president of the Philippines during his lifetime. Arum, in recent years, must have anointed Pacquiao. Whether or not Arum braces his enabling foresight on him with an illuminating hit of blessing, Pacquiao is sure not to consult with a medium.

Pacquiao may have just made an incredible facelift at the downward slope of his personal crisis in what could have been a corrective measure of his unrighteousness, admitting his gambling activities but downplaying his womanizing tendencies, as reported.

But, unlike most of the illustrious icons in the Philippines such as former President Joseph Estrada, former President Gloria Macapagal-Arroyo and more, he is by far spearheading a revival of justification by bible studies, igniting vigorous controversy, in fact, if Pacquiao is indeed "the enlightened," if not "the anointed one," by faith.

Pacquiao says he plans to use his stature in boxing to preach God's word. But, he says he would make a major announcement on a religious note later this month. And one thing remains uncertain: Pacquiao did not give a date as to when "God" wants him to retire.

Pacquiao is all ready to nullify Luke 6:29, as stated, "If someone strikes you on one cheek, turn to him the other also. If someone takes your cloak, do not stop him from taking your tunic." This, conversely, Pacquiao won't give Timothy Bradley a chance to smack his other check once he gets hit first. Inside the ring of the MGM Grand Arena in Las Vegas on June 9, Pacquiao frames his thought: "I will do my work inside the ring." One would wonder if Pacquiao would have that illuminating power on such occasion being "the anointed and enlightened one."

PACQUIAO CHOOSES HIGHER BID FOR POPULARITY

FEBRUARY 13, 2012 – WBO Welterweight Champion and Philippine Congressman Manny Pacquiao knows that a profession of religion has become popular with the world. In fact, "rulers, politicians, lawyers, doctors, merchants, join the church as a means of securing the respect and confidence of society and advancing their worldly interests," according to the book of the Great Controversy.

Amidst his declining popularity and his tumultuous relationship with his wife Jinky, even without rendering a detailed confession to the public, Pacquiao seeks to cover all his unrighteous acts under the garb, as offered by the Catholic Church of the Philippines, of "Bible Ambassador."

Sure, reciprocity exists here in terms of promotional values. Just like any other religious bodies, enforced by the wealth and influence of these baptized worldlings, they make a higher bid for popularity and patronage. I just hope these priests surrounding Pacquiao have not "broken their solemn vows of allegiance and fidelity to the King of Heaven."

But, Pacquiao's standing before God is one that no man could be in the right position to judge. Only God knows the condition of his heart. What is appealing to many is that Pacquiao's public witnessing about his relationship with God is influencing his close associates and fans that have not come to Christ for repentance and forgiveness. Even then, Pacquiao must publicly admit based on truth what he publicly denies. Humbly confessing one's "sins" by the power of the Holy Spirit, even to the point of tarnishing one's own public image and even to the point of self-incriminating to potential imprisonment, is the mark of a transformed man. And that's the true test of his faith.

What about potentially inflicting brain injury and castigating Timothy Bradley on June 9 at the MGM Grand Arena in Las Vegas, Nevada? Isn't this a gruesome prospect for one who has professed to be a born-again Christian?

Some of Pacquiao's fans e-mailed this writer, saying they would truly appreciate what Pacquiao, who claims to have become a born-again Christian, is doing now if he so publicly confesses his "sins" including boldly claiming how many children he has fathered and to name the names of the mothers of these children as a matter of confession to give justice to the truth. They also say he would be truly credible if he withdrew his investments from cockpit arenas and in other worldly affairs of men.

But, what's most revealing about Pacquiao is that he has provided a powerful evidence of God's work in him. His willingness to submit to Christ is what counts in the transformation of his character. If God had so changed the worst of sinner's heart, he can do the same with Pacquiao's.

Like Solomon of Old, Pacquiao's conversion may not be instantaneous. Tellingly his Christian experience can be one worth-studying. But, advancing, nevertheless, one's popularity with a "church" stinks. It's like prostituting the church in the highest form. So the public may pray for revelation.

PRELUDE TO MY CONTROVERSIAL ARTICLE: UNDER OBAMA, AMERICA BECOMING GOMORRAH

MAY 7, 2012 – President Barrack Obama may have just been cornered with the recent pronouncement of Vice President Joe Biden on the gay marriage issue, which Biden went ahead to declare his stance favoring gay marriage as a matter of human rights. Obama, though, preempted Biden's pronouncement, saying that he is on the same page with him, ready to make public his endorsement on same-sex marriage. His endorsement is unprecedented from a sitting president, which can be one of the most effective tools to get the votes from gays and human rights activists across the land.

While the beneficiaries of the said endorsement celebrate, the larger conservative populace and especially the Christian world and the Catholic Church must have been ignited with their might for moral defense against same sex marriage.

"The immorality issue of endorsing gay marriage might just become a stumbling block of Obama's bid to get reelected in the mid-term elections," says one admirer of Obama who has now considered not voting for him. "Obama cannot just take the heat of resisting the power of Sodom and Gomorrah of Old, which God had destroyed because of rampant of immorality and unrepentant hearts of gays and lesbians engaging in the sexual acts and worship."

"Is that what he teaches his children?"

"He has just become the catalyst for the destruction of the moral society of America, to which we are called upon to uphold good values and not destruction of family tradition based on biblical principles that this great land of America is built on," says Jackie Harris who claims to have mothered a gay but proud of her son being able to control his tendency to give-in to the sinful nature of engaging in same sex and, worse, same sex marriage.

Harris continues: "Obama is such an abominable figure of America. His ideals do not match the wishes of the framers of the United States Constitution. He is simply a curse to the man's foolishness. He is playing fire with Satan and his evil angels."

Obama may have just been less truthful all along by not telling the public his clear stance on the gay marriage issue. It's like Biden caught him off-guard. And now Obama has no choice but to get in line with Biden's pronouncement, or he would be endangered of not getting a great number of support from the massive liberal segment of the Democratic Party.

Even then, Obama might just have fired up religious leaders of both the Muslim and Jewish communities to abandon support for his presidential bid for a second term. They have been vocal of their stance against same sex marriage since the foundation of their faith and practices. But, same sectors have yet to comment on the same issue, as of this writing.

Meanwhile, the wide ranging coalition of protestant and Catholic faithful have been planning a comprehensive campaign not to support Obama's candidacy and his campaign for same sex marriage all across the land, according to a report from the Catholic's elite circle here in the U.S.

"Obama's conviction is simply not grounded with morality and fortitude that our society needs, most especially in this darkest hour of U.S. history," says one Catholic Bishop in California who prefers at this time not to make his name public until a public pronouncement is made by the higher authority of the mother church in the Vatican.

FOLLOW-UP, MAY 16, 2012: BIASED WRITERS GROSSLY TWISTED PACQUIAO'S VIEW ON SAME-SEX MARRIAGE

USA Today writer Tom Weir wrote on Saturday, May 14, 2012, "Manny Pacquiao challenges Obama on same-sex marriage", a fatal twist of the report I had written centering on an interview: "Pacquiao rejects Obama's new twist on the Scriptures."

In his article, Weir said "Pacquiao also **invoked** the Old Testament, and **recited** Leviticus 20:13, saying: 'If a man lies with a man as one lies with a woman, both of them have done what is detestable. They must be put to death; their blood will be on their own heads,'" referencing my fourth paragraph which states: "Pacquiao's directive for Obama calls societies to fear God and not to promote sin, inclusive of same-sex marriage and cohabitation, notwithstanding what Leviticus 20:13 has been pointing all along: 'If a man lies with a man as one lies with a woman, both of them have done what is detestable. They must be put to death; their blood will be on their own heads.'" **That, Pacquiao never said nor recited, nor invoked and nor did he ever refer to such context. And such context is not a "modern time context," however radical such contrast as a matter of point in the story of Leviticus, depicting God's perfect law before Moses of Old and its consequential measure to the Israelites during those times.**

Another over-board one who somehow reads Weir's point of interest is Dennis Romero of LA Weekly, and wrote: "Manny Pacquiao Says Gay Men Should Be 'Put to Death,'" dated May 15, 2012. **Such an article, I believe, carries unfair, convoluted remarks, as a matter of opinion.**

And as we see, **nowhere in my supposition and integration of my interview with Pacquiao did I mention that Pacquiao recited this Leviticus 20:13 nor did I imply that Pacquiao had quoted such.** I have simply reminded in my column how God made it clear in the Old Testament time that such practice of same-sex marriage is detestable and strictly forbidden, in as much as God wants to encourage his people practices that lead to health and happiness and fullness of life. As my style of literary writing suggests in almost all of my columns, the critical thoughts I tied up in the structure of thoughts I wanted to convey pertinent to this issue at hand do not translate Pacquiao's point of view, however conservative I am in my exposition.

And the same text has now been grossly misconstrued and regarded as Pacquiao's text, that which is not.

I hereby demand both Weir and Romero to apologize to Pacquiao. They, being writers for USA Today and LA Weekly respectively, should have a better reading comprehension than I do, rhetorically.

Though I am critical of Pacquiao in some way, I strongly commend Pacquiao's standing relative to same-sex marriage issue as only that has bearing to the morality side. What I see in him is a man who accepts everyone, regardless of sexual orientation. It's just he has been so vocal about some issues, inclusive of the Reproductive Health Bill which he does not support and remains pending for potential passage in the Congress of the Philippines, symbolic of his conservative stance regardless of political boundaries, which I surely admire. I believe while Pacquiao delves into his core, newfound faith in the conservative view of the Scriptures, he is as well a tolerant and a people-oriented believer.

Even then, I sincerely apologize for the confusion my column has caused. I certainly do not represent Pacquiao or his team. It's just Pacquiao's view and my column will always be unacceptable to a liberal world, most especially during this crucial period of U.S. President Barrack Obama's bid for second term and relative to his endorsement for the legalization of same-sex marriage which has met tremendous criticisms, oppositions and disenchantments across the U.S., as he gears up for the US Presidential Elections this November 2012.

The foregoing are top six responses to my controversial article, with citations. My purpose of citing the outstanding works of Michelle Malkin of Creators Syndicate, Mary Elizabeth Williams of Salon.com and Charles Jay of Boxing Insider, is to give more light to the justice that was denied relative to the exposition of truth and fairness affecting the substance of my literary piece being debated worldwide.

No. 1 Response by Michelle Malkin, Creators Syndicate on May 18, 2012

Headline: *"Bigoted Anti-Bigots: How The Gay-Marriage Mob Slimed Manny Pacquiao"*

"Boxing champion Manny Pacquiao is guilty — of being true to his Catholic faith. The gay-marriage mob is guilty — of the very ugly bigotry it claims to abhor. And left-wing media outlets are guilty — of stoking false narratives that shamelessly demonize religion in the name of compassion. The attempted crucifixion of Pacquiao this week was fueled by an online army of cultural shakedown artists, generously funded by billionaire George Soros and other so-called progressive philanthropists."

"Publications including USA Today, LA Weekly and Village Voice all ran outraged pieces on Pacquiao's 'homophobic' calls for violence. But, it was the interviewer, not Pacquiao, who made the citation. Ampong demanded apologies on behalf of Pacquiao. Feckless professional journalists blamed Ampong for their own biased reading and then grudgingly 'clarified' the truth in buried updates."

Note: To read the entire article, visit Michelle Malkin at Creators Syndicate via online.

No. 2 Response by Charles Jay, Boxing Insider on May 25, 2012

Headline: *"How the LGBT Groups Used Manny Pacquiao's 'Gay Marriage' Controversy To Further Agenda"*

"Of course, Gay Marriage USA, which established this poll, hadn't done a very good job at reading Granville Ampong's story in the National Conservative Examiner very carefully, or didn't care whether there was an ambiguity to it, as long as there could be some inference drawn. In less than two days, they gathered 4868 virtual signatures from people who apparently didn't care very much either. Where was the "hate speech"?

"If Pacquiao had really advocated stoning homosexuals to death, that may have constituted hate speech. But he really didn't say that at all, a point that was clarified by Ampong, and Pacquiao himself took great pains to establish that he wasn't thinking in that direction. Ampong made this clear in a follow-up: ". . . .nowhere in my supposition and integration of my interview with Pacquiao did I mention that Pacquiao recited this Leviticus 20:13 nor did I imply that Pacquiao had quoted such. I have simply reminded in my column how God made it clear in the Old Testament time that such practice of same-sex marriage is detestable and strictly forbidden, in as much as God wants to encourage his people practices that lead to health and happiness and fullness of life." Yet they still continued to collect signatures. When it became patently obvious that there was a big mistake, the "oops!" moment took place, and at least to their credit, the poll was shut down."

Note: To read the entire article, visit Charles Jay at Boxing Insiders via online.

No. 3 Response by Gareth Davies, The Telegraph - London on May 18, 2012

Headline: *"Manny Pacquiao Corrects Himself: Gay Is Fine; Gay Marriage Is Bad"*

"Pacquiao was not quoted in the Examiner story as making the biblical reference, but some American news outlets followed up by reporting that Pacquiao had used those lines."

Note: To read the entire article, visit Gareth Davies at The Telegraph via online.

No. 4 Response by Mary Elizabeth Williams of Salon.com on May 16, 2012

Headline: *"Manny Pacquiao Doesn't Want You Dead."*

"You see, within the original Examiner.com piece, Ampong went off on a bit of biblical tangent. "Pacquiao's directive for Obama calls societies to fear God and not to promote sin, inclusive of same-sex marriage and cohabitation," he wrote, "notwithstanding what Leviticus 20:13 has been pointing all along: "If a man lies with a man as one lies with a woman, both of them have done what is detestable. They must be put to death; their blood will be on their own heads."
That's Ampong. Quoting Leviticus.
"You could go ahead and infer that this is what Pacquiao was alluding to in his remarks, and you definitely could say that's some convoluted writing there. But Pacquiao himself clearly didn't issue the quote. But let's not let the barest understanding of attribution get in the way of a sensational headline, shall we? Before you could say gross perversion of the facts, Change.org was running a petition asking Nike to drop "homophobic boxer Manny Pacquiao," declaring, "In

an interview published Tuesday, March 15th with the conservative Examiner newspaper, the world-famous boxer and Los Angeles resident quoted Leviticus. . ." And except for the fact that Pacquiao didn't quote Leviticus, Examiner.com is not a conservative newspaper, and the interview didn't run on Tuesday, sure."

"I get that nobody really pays attention to what anybody posts on Examiner.com, but seriously. If you're going to quote someone, read the damn source material already. You need to have an eighth-grade reading proficiency level to get a driver's license, yet apparently you can be functionally illiterate and work for L.A. Weekly and USA Today. "

"On Wednesday, Granville Ampong wrote a follow-up post on the matter, saying of the Leviticus quote, "Pacquiao never said nor recited, nor invoked and nor did he ever refer to such context." And Pacquiao likewise issued a statement, saying, "I didn't say that, that's a lie. . . I didn't know that quote from Leviticus because I haven't read the Book of Leviticus yet," and adding, "I'm not against gay people . . . I have a relative who is also gay. We can't help it if they were born that way. What I'm critical of are actions that violate the word of God. I only gave out my opinion that same-sex marriage is against the law of God."

". . . Dennis Romero added more fuel to the mythic Pacquiao interview story Tuesday, in a piece headlined "Manny Pacquiao Says Gay Men Should Be 'Put to Death.'" USA Today then jumped in, reporting that "Pacquiao also invoked Old Testament, and recited Leviticus 20:13, saying: "If a man lies with a man as one lies with a woman." And the Village Voice blog, for good measure, reported, "The Bible Via-Manny Pacquiao: Gays Shouldn't Get Married, They Should Be 'Put To Death.'" How ridiculous did the whole thing get? On Pacquiao's own "official" website Tuesday, writer Keith Terceira said, "Manny Pacquiao was recently quoted in the USAToday as invoking the old testament." [sic]

Note: To read the entire article, visit Mary Elizabeth Williams at Salon.com via online.

No. 5 Response by Andrew Blankstein and Lance Pugmire, Los Angeles Times on May 17, 2012

Headline: *"Grove Bans Pacquiao Over Misrepresented Gay Marriage Comments"*

"Pacquiao was not quoted in the story as making the biblical reference. But he was reported as doing so by some American news outlets."

Note: To read the entire article, visit Andrew Blankstein and Lance Pugmire of the Los Angeles Times via online.

No. 6 Response by Kevin Iole of Yahoo!Sports on May 18, 2012

Headline: *"Skip Bayless, Stephen A. Smith Completely Blow It On Manny Peculiar Case, But Cast The Blame On Others"*

"Stephen A. Smith and Skip Bayless spent a few minutes toward the end of Wednesday's edition of "First Take" on ESPN roughing up boxer Manny Pacquiao. They had their facts incorrect, and they shredded Pacquiao for comments he didn't make."

"The blogosphere that Bayless and Smith railed upon made them look like a pair of two-bit journalists hardly worthy of the prestigious positions they hold."

"While reporters who care about small things like facts and accuracy went out, dug into the story and uncovered the truth, Smith and Bayless revealed themselves in the apologies as nothing more than a pair of bloviating, self-righteous boobs."

Note: To read the entire article, visit Kevin Iole at Yahoo!Sports via online.

Brian Livingston and Manny Pacquiao;
Taken on May 7, 2012 in Las Vegas, Nevada.
**Exclusive Copyright@2012 by Brian Livingston
for PACQUIAO UNDER CROSSFIRE.**

EXCLUSIVE INTERVIEW: REVEALING THE NEW MANNY PACQUIAO WITH PASTOR JERIC SORIANO

MAY 22, 2012 – *After visiting Manny Pacquiao at the Charles Turner landmark in Griffith Park last May 14 (Monday), I left the said site heading for an invitation by Engineer Ronnie Lu of Time Warner, to have breakfast with Team Pacquiao's security group. I was told Pacquiao's priest (sic) would be there with us. Thereupon, I exclusively interviewed Jeric Soriano, son of Genis Soriano (screen name: Nestor de Villa), who is Pacquiao's spiritual advisor, at the Denny's Restaurant on Sunset Boulevard in Hollywood. As known, this is status-post of the publication date of my controversial piece, "Pacquiao rejects Obama's new twist on the Scripture and tells him: 'God's words first,"* which I put on live via Examiner.com at about 1:00 a.m. here in Los Angeles, California (Pacific Time), on May 12 (Saturday). That was the third time I encountered Soriano but never had a conversation with him. Our conversation lasted about forty-five minutes.*

Perhaps Soriano is one of the most articulate ministers I've ever met in the evangelical circles. His countenance has shown much grace just as much as his manner of speaking. A sincere and a down-to-earth truth-seeker, Soriano is a son of a famous Filipino film producer of the Philippines. In an exclusive interview, Soriano describes Pacquiao as a "Christ-centered believer, evolving and learning - 'independently' - the ways of the Kingdom of God."

"I say 'independently' because I don't have to preach to him. I just show him the specific verses and he studies them with the inspiration of the Holy Spirit," Soriano said.

Soriano, who believes that "rapture" can happen anytime to any true believer of Jesus Christ before the seven years of the Great Tribulation, that is before the "Second Coming," said he sees Pacquiao as a genuine faithful of the Gospel truth. But, he did not say of the possibility of Pacquiao getting "raptured" any time even during or before his fight against undefeated Timothy Bradley on June 9 next month at the MGM Grand Arena in the Sin City of Nevada.

Soriano, on the other hand, had not confirmed yet, as of this writing, as to whether Pacquiao has reached that point of believing about his subscribed interpretation of the so-called "rapture." He said Pacquiao will have such eventual revelation about it as he studies the Scripture, day and night. But, "I believe Manny (Pacquiao) is true to his newfound faith," said Soriano. "He was once a radical sinner; he told me 'You name it, I did it.'"

"He is a radical sinner but radically saved in Jesus Christ," said Soriano. "He hates sin. But, he loves the sinner." Soriano continued: "He hates whatever bad deeds he committed. So whatever he is telling to himself, he is also sharing the same good news to others. Sure, he is telling himself: I don't want to go back."

Soriano said he believes Pacquiao is focusing on his identity in Jesus Christ: His righteousness. "Manny (Pacquiao) is not focusing on his sins in the past; he is rather focusing on the righteousness of Jesus Christ," he added.

Asked if Pacquiao's spiritual journey, being questioned by many political observers and other skeptics, has something to do with repackaging his public image which has been blighted by his past misdoings such as womanizing, gambling, drinking and other behavioral issues, Soriano said: "If ever I sense Manny (Pacquiao) has that suspected hidden political agenda, I would not support his cause. I rather pack-up and go home, anytime."

Soriano said he believes Pacquiao is an anointed one, to preach the Gospel of Jesus Christ most especially during this Earth's darkest hour. "Look at the signs of the times: the US President (Barrack Obama) has just approved (sic) gay marriage; You know that, you've done your research," said Soriano.

But, Soriano believes the Levitical laws and all the ceremonial ordinances, inclusive of one which became the center of debates in recent days, specifically Leviticus 20:13, had been nailed on the cross when Jesus was crucified at Mount Calvary about more than two thousand years ago.

He said Pacquiao, like he does, believes what Mark 12:30 says:"Love the Lord your God with all your heart and with all your soul and with all your mind and with all your strength." And Soriano took one step further from what Pacquiao believes and practices, according to Mark 12:31: "Love your neighbor as yourself."

Soriano said Jesus summed up all the laws in these two commandments. "We cannot obey these commandments without Jesus Christ," said Soriano. "And, Manny (Pacquiao) understands and believes that."

Meanwhile, Soriano, in a low but spirited tone, claimed he belongs to a church in Manila called New Life Christian Center. "If you come to our church, you will not sign any papers, or anything for membership. You are free to come in. You're free to go. Our church is all based about having that relationship with Jesus Christ, our Creator, Lord and Savior," he added.

Soriano said Pacquiao and Pacquiao's wife, Jinkee, and a few company, are tentatively scheduled June 16 to leave for Israel on a spiritual tour with Top Rank Promoter Robert "Bob" Arum.

EXCLUSIVE UPDATE: REVEALING THE NEW MANNY PACQUIAO WITH BRIAN LIVINGSTON

MAY 7, 2012: HOLLYWOOD, CALIFORNIA – Nestled in one of Los Angeles County's most picturesque settings, Griffith Park has been synonymous with Hollywood since its institution of Griffith Observatory in 1935 and official marking of Mount Hollywood in 1923. This mountain is, by far, the most popular hiking trail in all of Griffith Park. One of the reasons for its popularity is the access to a million dollar view of Los Angeles, including the Pacific Ocean and eastern San Fernando Valley, sprawling more than four thousand acres and it is the largest publicly owned park in the United States.

A part of it is the famous Mount Hollywood Hiking Trail. It has an elevation of 1,626 feet but considerably yields a consistent elevation of ten to forty-five degrees. The distance round trip from Fern Dell trail is five miles, from the Charlie Turner Trailhead at the Observatory the distance is two and a half miles round trip.

Today is a gorgeous, cool and breezy day. The sun was at an angle of about 45 degrees, teasing the deep ridge by the Hollywood sign with less hazy skies right above and across the hills and the plains.

At least, that's what I saw from where I paid my visit this 8:30 a.m. And no thickening cloud was seen, not even a transient sweeping trace of atmospheric smog, perfecting 65 degrees Fahrenheit. And the familiar whistle of blue jays that penetrated the thin air somewhere around was such the welcoming one just when I arrived at the parking lot of the Griffith Observatory in Los Angeles overlooking the great metropolis, about four miles from my residence.

I felt refreshed by the Spring breeze and familiar perfumes from the flower beds and Eucalyptus trees, sort of signaling a new shift for my field work after four months of not visiting this awesome place. What was rather more familiar was the usual resurrecting throng there which had been ritually visiting in recent years. In some way, they must have given Manny Pacquiao, the most influential pugilist on the earth today, the warm reception and admiration he needed. He still comes up here for his most challenging preparation for this June 9 encounter against undefeated light welterweight champion, Timothy Bradley, who is currently deep in his training up in Indio, about 75 miles away from Pacquiao's rallying point, the Charles Turner's landmark of Hollywood.

Nonetheless, another mark of old that still lingered was the usual goofing around, as a matter of pass time, by some of the rambunctious, less-informed disciples and sycophants, otherwise known as the L.A. Boys – who are Filipinos but non-Cebuano-speaking ones – even in the midst of interviews seemingly disturbing and somewhat exhibiting classic hangover behavior, and, worse, with cheap shots of boisterous jokes, as if suffering from attention-deficit disorder.

But it's calming in fact, seeing the same faces from Team Pacquiao, except a new one, though unconfirmed as I was only told he is Pacquiao's brother-in-law. Pacquiao had just finished his morning jog. My good friend, Chino Trinidad of GMA-7 from the Philippines, had just started his live interview with Pacquiao.

In his white sweat shirt printed with green letters on the front side that read "FIGHT FOR A BETTER WORLD", and red short pants (both of which carried the MP sign), Pacquiao stood by the passenger front door of Team Pacquiao's SUV, while my wife, Mary Jane, was filming the same scene, just for fun, from a considerable distance, not intending to disrupt what's taking place at such moment. Pacquiao looked upbeat, yet with intermittent gesture of meditation before his fans, some of them egging him to sign his autograph on an assortment of pieces of remembrance they brought. Looking tired, and maybe just tired of getting tired, he turned away no one who came on time. Behind the crowd, I got hold of Pacquiao's friend Brian Livingston, manager of the Nike Outlet here in Los Angeles, who was with Pacquiao in Baguio City serving voluntarily as Pacquiao's jogging partner.

Livingston, a professional marathoner and a philosopher in his own right, shared his thoughts as to how amazed he is at what's going on with Pacquiao. Asked about his assessment of his recent journey to the Philippines, Livingston said: "Journey is a great word. It was twenty-one days in the Philippines. It was a great training camp in that not only were we able to get Manny started, but it was just great personally for me because I was able to meet so many new people. And even I got a stronger connection to boxing by training there and starting my own little regimen."

**Exclusive Copyright@2012 by Brian Livingston
for PACQUIAO UNDER CROSSFIRE.**
Flawless synchronicity by Brian Livingston and Manny Pacquiao as they seemed to be skimming airborne upon the dusty lane of Mt. Hollywood Hiking Trail at Berlin Forest in Griffith Park of Los Angeles, California. Taken on May 19, 2012.

Livingston spent longer runs with Pacquiao every Monday, Wednesday and Friday, and shorter ones on Tuesdays, Thursdays and Saturdays just to loosen up – days when Pacquiao would have his sparring sessions dealt with. Livingston said he thought Baguio City, because of its elevation, is a little bit cooler obviously than it is in Los Angeles this time, and the air is also cleaner. "And it was pretty nice because we went up there very early in the morning," he added.

"There were a few times when he cramped up. But we've been trying some new things such as trigger-point device, massage, and rolling out using the same trigger-point device, which all seem to help."

"Manny is also a little bit more mature in the way he's approaching his training, progressively working into a run, rather than starting out really fast, and cramping." Livingston continued: "There might be a nutritional element and that's probably the last frontier that needs to be approached. And then I think there's a mental aspect as well that needs to be explored. I think when you get it into your head that you will have cramps, you actually will soon get tired and develop cramps. And it comes to your senses often, making it much easier to happen every subsequent time and it gets even worse. God willing, Manny didn't cramp today. The less that happens, the more confident he becomes in his training. I think we can put that issue of cramps to rest."

"I think Manny said it best when he expressed that he wants to have a strong spirit in connection to his strong body. He's really focused on his biblical study, to really feed, and to really nourish his spirit. That's the biggest change I've seen [in him] when it comes to his enthusiasm. He's really tying his spiritual growth to the growth of his performance," Livingston said.

Livingston, himself a Christian, said he participates in bible studies with Manny, and would still love to do it mostly because he is interested in how it translates into performance. "I think it's really important that you have that time to meditate and really get connected to God who is authentic to you," said Livingston.

He said he believes what Pacquiao had said to everyone: "It's not about the church, it's not about religion. It's about your connection to Jesus Christ."

"And that's what my mission is – in all my bible studies," Livingston added. "You cannot win a fight with just your body; you need the spirit," he continued. Livingston said he sees further the much-deeper dimension of Pacquiao: "He does not jog with headphones anymore and just shuts the world around him. He is more receptive now. He communes with nature. He is genuinely charismatic."

Meanwhile, the sun still asserted its righteousness with the morning heat that was perhaps above 65 degrees Fahrenheit now, just when Livingston bid to dismiss my brief engagement with him as Team Pacquiao was about to leave. Pacquiao was still accommodating a few late-comers for his autograph signing. I just thought I got what I needed for the day and onward: another wisdom of the Ancient of Days.

My wife, being contented with what she got from her little filming, signaled from the far right of the Charles Turner's landmark that we must leave now for breakfast, cancelling our plan to jog to the mountaintop. Not more than two minutes, Team Pacquiao left the site, leaving one soul pondering as he wrote this piece.

The author is interviewing Joel Diaz, trainer of Timothy Bradley, at the Beverly Hills Hotel in Beverly Hills California. Diaz thought "Pacquiao needs to knock out Bradley," to be convincing of his supremacy. Diaz trained Bradley at the Indio's Boys and Girls club of America in California.
Exclusive Copyright@2012 by PACQUIAO UNDER CROSSFIRE
for Manny Pena. Far left is Joseph Pimentel from Asian Publications

The author is interviewing Top Rank Godfather Robert "Bob" Arum at Fortune Gym on Sunset Boulevard in Hollywood, California. Taken in 2011.
Exclusive Copyright@2012 by PACQUIAO UNDER CROSSFIRE
for Engineer Ronnie Lu & family

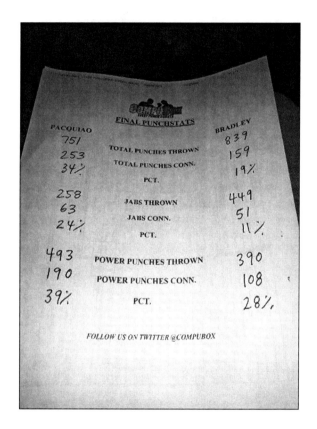

*Official final punch stats of Compubox
from Pacquiao-Bradley fight on June 9, 2012.*
Exclusive photo copyright @ 2012 by PACQUIAO UNDER CROSSFIRE
for Engineer Ronnie Lu & his family

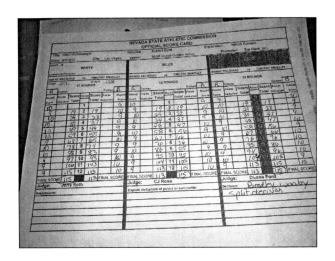

The Nevada State Athletic Commission official score card of the board of judges for Pacquiao-Bradley fight on June 9, 2012.
Exclusive photo copyright @ 2012 by PACQUIAO UNDER CROSSFIRE
for Engineer Ronnie Lu & his family

***Exclusive Copyright@2012 by* PACQUIAO UNDER CROSSFIRE**
for Manny Pena; Taken at the Beverly Hills Hotel in Beverly Hills, California during Pacquiao-Bradley Press Conference in February 2011.

INTRICACY OF BRADLEY'S VICTORY OVER PACQUIAO

JUNE 9, 2012 – Several experts' opinions may have blighted the integrity of the Pacquiao-Bradley fight's board of judges and of Top Rank Godfather Robert "Bob" Arum's reflexive role on Timothy Bradley as the new WBO Welterweight Champion.

The attacks on Arum and on the two judges, CJ Ross and Duane Ford, who both scored 115-113 for Bradley, respectively, are still raging potentially in cosmic proportion. The other judge, Jerry Roth, who was one of the three judges who officiated during the Oscar de la Hoya versus Tito Trinidad fight in 1999 and one who scored 115-113 in favor of Trinidad, conversely scored 115-113 for Manny Pacquiao over Bradley. In the De La Hoya-Trinidad fight, Trinidad started landing some powerful right hands which he was missing in the early rounds, just like in the case of Bradley, and relentlessly continued pursuing De La Hoya in the 10th, 11th and 12th. Unlike De La Hoya, Pacquiao did not run away from Bradley's harm despite being so ineffective; his showing of strength was remarkable, even then.

Meanwhile, from Bradley's corner last night, he was pushed to keep attacking Pacquiao, appearing as if he had gained composure. In the late rounds, Bradley knew he could make it close, and he kept attacking and found some successes, indeed, regardless of whether Pacquiao let him do the same under his mercy.

For these two judges who are in question by the majority, Pacquiao was not doing well in the last five to six rounds – just like in the case of De la Hoya who gave away the late rounds to Trinidad. It's more than the scorecards and the punch statistics. Sure, judges have criteria to follow other than the scorecards such as clear defense, ring generalship, aggression, and clear punches. From the perspective of these two judges, Pacquiao fell short of those criteria to retain his title, at least in the last five out of six rounds.

What these judges might have seen was that Pacquiao did better in the last four rounds against Marquez than against Bradley. Like other boxing pundits, Jerome Laquinon, a critical boxing observer based in Canada, said: "I read lots of articles today and they are all against the judges of the fight. . . even the master himself blamed it on the judges; I'm talking about Bob Arum here, the master of conspiracy."

Let's review the tape of the Pacquiao-Bradley fight from rounds 8 through 12 and see if Pacquiao was really effective. Check the trend and the pattern. Notice: Pacquiao became less active, and had relinquished his ring generalship and good defense to Bradley's effective frontal attacks. Pacquiao's clear punches and effective aggression diminished. Bradley effectively disrupted Pacquiao's rhythm. In fact, Bradley was more resilient, rising up much stronger than in the early rounds, which was more fundamental than just statistical drama.

In other words, it's all about Bradley's resiliency versus statistics which balanced out with the established boxing criteria. And that's why judging will always be a subjective experience. An unwarranted theory surfaced, noting that Pacquiao was being too merciful, intimating the prospect that he could have knocked Bradley out in the early rounds had Pacquiao been really intent to execute the purported game plan.

But Pacquiao's ability to deliver clearer punches may have been a factor even in the early rounds, however punch-stat revealed otherwise. His accuracy was less of a knuckle-head explosion. Bradley's punches were more pronounced in rounds 8, 9, 10, 11 and 12.

Should Ross and Ford be blamed for Pacquiao's performance in late rounds?

For Arum, it's all victory for him. Floyd Mayweather, Jr., seen by several boxing experts; as the remaining pugilist who can truly destroy Pacquiao, if not the other way around, might become a negligible figure on Pacquiao's final fights before retirement. Pacquiao might just have two more matches left: against Bradley this fall, and against Juan Manuel Marquez in the spring of 2013. Bradley's victory — call it a conspiracy?

Only Arum, these two judges – Ross and Ford – their cohorts and the celestial beings know.

PACQUIAO'S TOP 10 SECRETS OF SUCCESS REVEALED

Exclusive Copyright @ 2012 by **PACQUIAO UNDER CROSSFIRE**
for Salven Lagumbay

The three critical players of modern boxing history of the Philippines: boxing legend-turned-actor-Congressman Emmanuel "Manny" Pacquiao plotting a move against Grandmaster Dong Secuya, CEO of the famous Pacland and Philboxing.com, and Salvin Lagumbay, Board-certified boxing judge and the first ABC-certified Filipino international judge, contributing editor of Philboxing.com and columnist of the Inquirer Group of Publications, as the third party observer.

*A*UGUST 19, 2010 – Just like fire in his bones, Sarangani Congressman Emmanuel "Manny" Pacquiao's passion for success is rather exemplary and proverbial. He has penetrated ever increasingly the diverse segments of the world public of boxing. Despite odds and controversies, everything seems to go right with him, at least according to his own foresight. Even though his characters are not flawless, the Philippines look particularly bright each time he fights. For the oppressed, the suppressed and the repressed, Manny's thoughts and aura bring new life to the best of their inspiration. In fact, "Manny Pacquiao" and "inspiration," though distinguishable, have become seemingly inseparable in the hearts of the "less inspired many" and the "less informed" of the Maharlikan nation.

Not to be outdone, the same tenor of distinction sums up his top 10 principles of success in life:

1. Submission to the will of God Almighty and maximization of gift He has given: "One journalist asked Manny, *"Meron ka bang agimat?'* (Do you have an amulet?) And Manny said, *"Wala akong agimat. Ang alam ko, nagbibigay ng Diyos ng mga regalo sa tao. At ang binigay Niya sa akin, malakas akong sumuntok. Kaya ginagamit ko ito sa pagbigay ng kaluwalhatian sa Kanya . . ."* (I don't have an amulet. What I know is that God gives gifts to people. And He gave me the gift of a strong punch. I will use it to give glory to Him.") This is a loose quotation, but it captures the essence of what Pacquiao said." - *Excerpt from the writings of Bo Sanchez.*

Sanchez in his writing is reminded of another athlete who spoke about this same powerful principle. He cited Eric Liddell, Olympic champion sprinter, who said, "God made me fast, and when I run, I feel His pleasure. . ." (You can watch this inspiring story in the true-to-life movie, *Chariots of Fire*).

2. Health is wealth: Pacquiao says *"Alaga-an natin ang ating sarili; isa lang ang buhay natin."* (Let's take care of ourselves; we only have one life).

3. Focus and determination: Despite juggling different tasks and facing competing inroads, Pacquiao's mind is set on one goal in a moment's notice. He said: *"Pag naa na ko diha sa maong situasyon, akong himoon ang tanan nakong makaya hangtud sa katapusan."* (Once I am in that situation, I do everything I can to the end).

4. Play the crowd: While in the ring for a fight, Pacquiao sees to it not to disappoint what the crowd expects: an action-packed match. For him, being in the ring with another gladiator is "like lyrics in a melody of two spirited fighters." In his fight against Miguel Cotto and even Eric Morales, he showed his playfulness when he felt he needed to thrill the crowd at the expense of himself getting hurt. He allowed them to box him freely, and to get hit at nerve-wracking and even exasperating moments.

5. Sportsmanship: In an era where athletes are so self-centered, it's refreshing to see a story like Pacquiao's. His conduct and attitude are considered befitting in sports.

6. Power of forgiveness: Pacquiao believes in the healing power of forgiveness. He has shown unconditional forgiveness to his detractors and even to those who have pocketed some of his hard-earned money.

7. Power of giving: Pacquiao believes in the power of giving. He has retained less wealth than ever and gave more to charities, friends, and even to the less fortunate.

8. Expecting the unexpected: Even being so confident a person that he is, Pacquiao readies to face the worst event(s) that life can offer: *"Hindi talaga malaman kong anong mangyayari; tanggapin natin lahat at ating pasalamatan ang Dios."* (We really do not know what will happen; let's accept everything and let's give thanks to God).

9. "Let's move on. . ." perspective: Pacquiao's three losses based on his boxing record from the hands of Rustico Torrecampo (KO 3 in 1996), Medgoen Singsurat (KO 3 in 1999), and Erik Morales (UD in 2005) have never stopped him from pursuing his aim to move on.

10. Humility: Pacquiao's humility is one such character that resonates with his people. He would never assume he knows it all: "I am just a fighter, and only God knows what will happen in the ring."

PACQUIAO RISING TO A HIGHER LEVEL, NEARLY BECOMING LIKE HOWARD COSELL

MAY 2, 2012 – Don't be surprised if one day world boxing superstar Manny Pacquiao, like American sports journalist Howard Cosell, will emerge as one of the most outspoken opponents of boxing and crusade for the abolition of the sport. In his most recent interview with ANC, Manny revealed his most intriguing conviction about the sport: *"Sinasaktan mo 'yong kapwa' mo, so parang* [against the law of God]." ("You're hurting your fellowmen, so it's like you're going against the law of God").

Unlike Pacquiao, however, Howard Cosell was widely known for his blustery, cocksure personality. In one respect, Pacquiao does share a similarity. Not of intrinsic personality, Pacquiao is becoming like Cosell in terms of advocacy. Even though Cosell was not a boxer, his rise to international prominence was primary to his connection with boxing when he became the color commentator on ABC boxing broadcasts in the early 1960's.

Cosell became the unofficial "voice of boxing" in 1966 when he called the heavyweight title bout between Muhammad Ali and Karl Middleberger from Frankfurt, Germany. When "he continued calling fights for ABC until 1982, he became disgusted with the sport after calling a particularly brutal match between Larry Holmes and Randall "Tex" Cobb" in which Cobb took a terrible beating from Holmes as the referee failed to stop the fight even when Cobb appeared defenseless, according to Hillstrom writers and Roger Matuz.

Cosell then emerged from being the "voice of boxing" to becoming the "voice for the abolition of boxing". Just how Cosell began to understand the dangerous prospects of boxing which could involve injuries and even death, and how it started to be ingrained deeper in Pacquiao's mind, many are now seeing the "new Pacquiao" becoming like Cosell, most especially that he himself is a boxer who just had a "revelation" from his God about the dark side of boxing.

Pacmanian Sect Rising, To The Glory Of 'God' In The Highest

The modern Maharlikan icon finds his place in the Universe before the blazing yet glowing sun. With the passing grip and password, he has kept secret: his one of the most fascinating journeys that invokes a blessing from the "Architect of the Multiverses." In his heart, prudence directs his actions with obedience to the highest degree based on the code of conduct, an identifier of his persona. Every victory and defeat he shares from the ring of madness carries not only a symbolic meaning but a deeply psychological one as well that strikes the very hearts of the Maharlikans.

That's Manny Pacquiao who has become the catalyst of hope to the hopeless and to the downtrodden, at least in the midst of his meditation. And nothing could be further than the truth: His duty is not to himself but to his family and his fellowmen, his community and his country. That's why he has committed to do whatever he can to improve society and environment. In fact, he has helped found hospital(s) and funded schools and libraries. And for every calamity the Philippines has faced, he has dug deep into his pockets and donated to charities.

What impresses me most, nevertheless, about Pacquiao are his ways of reflecting the moral precepts to the fullest in his life. Since that defining moment in November of 2011 in which "God" spoke to him in a dream, Pacquiao says it made him "recommit himself to God." Because of this "encounter with God," he has become passionate about morality and welfare of humankind. And most important, his brotherly love and earnest regard to the truth have made him "tolerant in respecting the rights of others to hold beliefs that are different to his."

But what seems to stand behind Pacquiao is the belief of some Pacmanians that he has transcended the ordinary boundaries of human society by entering into a new realm of existence "in Christ," and that he has become spiritually superior. This idea is not an imminent expectation but is slowly becoming a reality. There will be intense arguments on this point in the media and in the circle of intelligentsia and illustrados, unless otherwise suppressed, repressed and oppressed by Pacquiao's spell. Money makes wonders, at least in this world we live.

As for now, nothing is less manipulative in emboldening the less- informed's state of depravity onto his glory. His acting field on TV shows would only derail the fortification of his newfound faith. They have depicted him as less natural, like an adulterated, nonsensical philanthropist. Such would only precipitate a whirlwind of diminishing power in the efficacy of his spiritual mission. No matter how sincere he is, TV shows would only become a catalyst of false hopes for the needy.

Outside of showbiz, however, Pacquiao's new and more radical forms of piety have arisen and have become noticeable. Even with the resulting increase in polarization along political, socioeconomic and ethnocultural lines, he still has closely aligned with reforming tendencies coming directly from his increased awareness of the Scripture. Yes, he takes on a new significant identity - a conservatively heightened sense of piety. This, for him, only serves as a unifying symbol for his spirituality and Maharlikan identiy, even to the point of producing excitement, if not anxiety, among proliferating groups of religious organizations in the Philippines. Pacquiao is becoming a formidable force in both spiritual and political realms.

Although his appeal is not restricted to sectarian worshippers, he nonetheless uses his charisma and wealth as tools for galvanizing certain forms of sectarian identity and spirit. In the process of redefining his self in the public eye, he may have conceived the kingship ideology of a secret society. Sure, in the mainstream American media, Pacquiao is suspected of being controlled by the hands of one of the earth's most powerful forces, a force that demands change for a time in the banner of morality and divine fortitude.

From this reflection came a note of expectation. Pacquiao has chosen to return to the ways of the "Architect of the Multiverses" through repentance and reformation. And for many of his worshippers, it only helps fuel the fire of idolatry. To some, this is not necessarily out of allegiance to the lordship of the true living God of the entire Multiverses. The same worshipers listen to Pacquiao's preaching and at the same time they cannot help themselves but worship the Maharlikan icon. With his spell, a diffusion of a "new kind of religion" exists, however ancient the "spirit" it embraces. It's sad when Pacquiao's followers have been enslaved by the same kind of "spirit." They mindlessly worship him. They would do anything to please him, buying his "image" in the form of any merchandise and embracing his "mark" as much as he pleases them with his charm and prestige. Pacquiao is NOT necessarily a devil. But those who worship him are certainly worshipping "the image and mark of the Beast," as much as they are being deceived.

Even then, in this period, the tensions between the Pacquiao die-hard followers and the Roman Catholic believers in the Maharlikan nation are now slowly growing stronger. New questions of self-definition have begun to emerge, especially in light of Pacquiao's increasing contact with the evangelical Christian ministers. The same stronger ties reflect Pacquiao's changing social horizons. We are beginning to see the Pacmanian movement breaking away from its Roman Catholic roots and becoming a separate institutional church, or what we may more properly call "Pacmanian sect." Another factor that becomes more apparent in this period is diversity among the faithful within the Pacmanian movement. But it would become a movement predominantly of converts from the Roman Catholic Church.

But how would this happen? How would this affect the Maharlikans who are caught in the middle of this momentous change, a societal change which will become inevitable?

One day we will begin to realize that the dynamism of the Pacmanian movement and even its complex textures and changes would eventually become clearer. I am neither an apocalyptic firebrand nor a social critic. But, Pacquiao's story - this story - will have to be told to future generations. Mine would just be one of the literary trajectories as newer stories will have to be retold in newer situations, as Pacquiao's emerging power inevitably sees a new opposing audience out of the Maharlikan conscience, at the crossroads of intellectualism. Mind you, Pacquiao Under Crossfire will have to be retold once more, at least at such time that we may otherwise lose in the twilight zone. And at the height of Pacquiao's political career, the Pacmanian movement will come of age socially and intellectually in the Maharlikan nation, at the behest of the "unseen hand" of the secret order.

As Pacquiao continues to grow as his fame increases in some way, I would not be surprised if he will become the president of the Philippines someday. And regardless of whose eye scrutinizing him, I pray that Pacquiao will always be a man of God. May the Creator of the Multiverses, in the name of Jesus Christ, our Lord and our Savior, continue to bless him and his family and ministry, forevermore.

Photojournalist-boxing commentator Leoncio "Leo" Royo with Pacquiao's childhood friend and boxing trainer, Buboy Fernandez. Taken at the Beverly Hills Hotel in Beverly Hills, California in 2010.
Exclusive photo copyright @ 2012 by PACQUIAO UNDER CROSSFIRE
for Gina Royo

Mariano Baltazar 'Mar' Vidal
Exclusive photo copyright @ 2012 by PACQUIAO UNDER CROSSFIRE
for Monalisa Vidal

BIGGER THAN THE BIG PICTURE

*P*erhaps he is larger than what the story of Emmanuel 'Manny' D. Pacquiao tells in his portrait. His name may be pretty isolated when you search it through the Google search engine. Worse, nothing about his sake would surface in spite of his immense credibility it supposes to bring. But Mariano Baltazar "Mar" Vidal, 56, humbly makes it right to immortalize his newfound hero of the Maharlikan nation.

"I am just very happy to paint Manny's image on a 40' x 60' canvas," said the homegrown talent who started painting at the age of four, out of his fascination to draw movie characters, such as James Bond or Hercules. "It's worth painting Pacquiao all because he has inspired the entire nation of the Philippines."

Vidal said: "I am just blessed that Manny chose me over other great painters. It so happened when he visited early last year at the Crown Regency Hotel here in Cebu (Philippines) where I had my works displayed, along with other good artists. He put his right arm around my shoulder, telling me that he was very impressed with my works of art."

A few months later after Manny's fight against Ricky Hatton in 2009, Mar received a text message early in the morning. Manny asked to see him at the Waterfront Hotel, just a few miles from his house. Manny made sure his visit in Cebu at such time would remain unnoticed by the media and other local dignitaries.

"*Bai* (Cebuano way of calling a friend), please make me a portrait," Mar recalled of Manny's appeal with his eternal boyishness. "How much does it cost?" Manny asked.

Mar, thus far, took the chance of a lifetime, and said: "Because you have given so much honor to our country, I will give it to you as a gift."

Mar, a devout Catholic, said he believes he is commissioned from above to inspire his countrymen and others by incorporating his gift of art to the uplifting of the image of his boxing idol. Nevertheless, it took Mar a little bit longer to finish his painting of Manny which, he said, could have been done in six to seven months. But it was all because of his two children's busy schedules in which he was proactively taking a part daily. His son, Izarzuri Vidal, an opera singer who won in a world competition, frequently participates in numerous concerts which Mar seldom misses. His daughter, Monalisa, a registered nurse in the Philippines who, like other Filipino nurses who aspire to go abroad specifically to American soil, was reviewing for the national licensure examination to become a registered nurse in the US. His wife, Gwendolyn, is a certified public account who works full-time six days a week at Union Bank in Lapu-Lapu City where they live. To sum up, Mar champions his life painting as well a better picture for his family like the fathers of old. And for his idol, he finished the painting in one full year.

"It's my pride and honor to have my artwork hanging-on your wall," recalled Mar telling Manny, referring to one of the walls in Manny's mansion in General Santos City. "This is not an ordinary painting."

The complexity of painting is one of a challenge. High quality oil-painting cannot be a onetime activity. It goes through four stages of coating, and possibly a longer drying period so that the finished piece would not crack. Even the famous Leonardo Da Vinci took more than 15 years to finish some of his paintings, and, for Michelangelo, decades, Mar recounted.

One spring time, Pacquiao, who knows how to appreciate paintings, appealed to Mar to teach him how to draw when he retires from boxing. "Can we be text-mates?" Manny asked Mar, referring to sending text messages via cellular phone.

Then Mar asked Manny to sign on his sketch book. In his usual friendly touch, Manny instead drew Mar's face jokingly as a caricature, and he wrote his cellular number below, said Mar, a multi-decorated graduate from the University of the Philippines - Cebu in 1980 with a bachelor's degree in fine arts, had received awards, scholarships, and other recognitions both from private and public organizations. After graduation, he was prompted to accept the offer to teach at the same institution, which he enjoyed doing for the next seven years.

Mar got high marks among the circle of the Philippine arts when he won first prize in the Visayan competition in the 1980's. He takes pride of his two protégés who have made it to the top: Monique Lhuillier, a world renowned fashion designer, has captured the taste of Jennifer Lopez who has become her own regular customer. Kenneth Cobonpue, a furniture designer, has disarmed Brad Pitt's curious eyes and Brad tapped him as his designer for some delicate works in the furnishings. Both students have made Mar more credible to the upscale art critics and buyers.

"I know Mar is a great artist. I have seen his actual paintings. They are fantastic," said Jocelyn Pepito who hails from Cebu and now resides in Los Angeles, California. "In fact, I have bought two portraits of the Blessed Virgin Mary which Mar painted; they are so beautiful; Mother Mary's eyes there look alive."

Mar, whose famous paintings of Monalisa and a few religious ones – some originally of Michelangelo's by-product of ingenuity, also won the hearts of the Vatican artwork authorities, in 1972 when Reverend Father Pertal was commissioned by Pope John Paul VI to search collectors' paintings for the Vatican Church. He sent a courtier around to find the best painter in Cebu. The courtier asked all the artists to give him a sample of their work to send to the Pope. He came to Mar's artwork as one of the candidates while the latter was still a high school student at the Abellana National High School, explained his mission, and asked him for a drawing which would give the Pope some idea of his competence and style. For Mar, that was such a formidable inspiration to him. In fact, his painting of a Cebuano Saint Cebuano Pedro Calungsod, the only Cebuano Saint beatified by Pope John Paul II in 2000, was commissioned by Msgr.

Chris Garcia. Finally, the same painting was brought to the Vatican in 2003 and can now be found at the world famous Gallery of Arts Museum of the Vatican Church.

Mar spent his primary years at the Zapatera Elementary School at Sikatuna Street in Cebu City where he saw the beginning of his life as an artist. He received many recognitions and awards and won first place in many contests until he graduated in 1969.

On May 1 last year, Mar's painting of Manny was finished. After drying it airborne to make it a perfect whole, Manny's close associate Rex "Wacky" Salud took it and presented the same to Manny at his mansion in General Santos City, Philippines. Manny gave Mar a monetary gift of an undisclosed amount. His paintings are priced thirty-thousand pesos and up.

Mar, though highly regarded by his folks and networks of artists and buyers, tones himself as a low profile artist. All his paintings are home-based. As soon as he starts painting, he shows no signs of slowing down from dawn to dusk when he is free from the usual mundane matters in his own dwelling. Much with an almost undetectable intensity and attention to detail, Mar still thrives with his family in a sunny disposition.

In that historic Island of Mactan where the heritage of arts and trade are still reminiscent of the Spanish regime, where the landmarks of illustrious cathedrals built and decorated by the Cebuanos with the works of uncommon artists whose names remain unwritten in the books, the inspiration for art may have not vanquished. In fact, art just woke up in Sangi, Lapu-lapu City. It is there, alive once more: Mar is simply a great genius.

Perhaps he has the amazing knack to put things in celestial perspective. "I pray all the time," Mar said of his maxim. His fortitude and philosophy are one of solemnity in prayer. He prays in total silence while he paints.

Perhaps Mar is bigger than the big picture.

COME FLY WITH ME

1st Place: International Speech Contest 2000 held at the Ron Hubbard Auditorium in Los Angeles, California
(A seven -minute speech, Copyright @ April 19, 2000)

Since my subject is about motivation, I declare, ladies and gentlemen, that this year is the era of motivation. Motivation is a sweeping generalization. But its cutting edge impact penetrates our better selves: our souls, our goals, aspirations and deepest yearnings.

We reached the moon, through our first American astronauts. Indeed, the mind of man – our minds – its incredible imagination, evidenced by the advances of technology, is awesome – buoyed by motivation. That makes the impossible, possible!

Just an illustration: the eaglet. This creature fell to the ground from the protective wings of the most powerful bird, the most feared predator of the horizon, the mother eagle. The eaglet learned to survive scratching the ground with a flock of chicks from the mother hen. Alas, one bright day, the mother eagle was visibly seen high in the horizon. Lo and behold, after several fly-by maneuvers, the eaglet saw its mother. By the masterstroke of derring-do, I call it conventional wisdom, its wings opened wide, it eyes popped up; it buoyed itself and up, up and away, left the earth and soared into the limitless skies. Yes, for an eaglet to learn how to fly is an instinct, but to reach the highest of the sky is motivation.

That, to me, was pure, unadulterated motivation.

We, from all the peoples of the earth, came to this land. We were motivated and lured by the invitation of the blindfolded lady on Ellis Island, New York, with this simple plea: "Give me your tired, your poor. . .," an open door policy to all. Biblically, immigrants come to this promised land of milk and honey – America!

In my case, I left my country to find a better life here. I was uprooted from the culture, from the nurturing of my father and mother, from the company of my loved ones and all. But, it is not at all a bed of roses. As Shakespeare said, my struggles here could be aptly described as the result of, and I quote, "the slings of outrageous fortune."

Please listen carefully. On June 17, 1994, my former district manager closeted me in his office: "Granville, your promotion will be effective on Monday."

Elated and upbeat, I hurriedly and gracefully replied, "Thank you, Sir."

"Here is a final check for you."

"A final check? Why?"

"Because we have confirmed reports that you are an illegal alien: UNDOCUMENTED!"

That moment of infamy devastated me. It was a bolt of lightning that rendered me a wretched soul. In my conscience, the "still small voice" got the better of me. I had to wrestle with a collision course of unforeseen circumstances. I rationalized: "Maybe my termination was based on the system of America on law and justice."

Still I followed my options. It was perhaps the easiest path for me to relieve my pain physically and mentally. I sought the aid of psychics, the assistance of quack-doctors and false prophets. I took refuge in bottles, alone in the corner of the bar. Finally, I realized I reached the so called "dead end" in my life. All my hopes and lofty aims to succeed in this country were relegated to the back burner. I was ready to give up.

"Giving up? Heck! Was that all there is?"

I lost my resources. No one dared to accept me for a job. I lost my self-esteem. One big solitary night. Loneliness enveloped my entire being. I imagined the mouth of the abyss waiting for an easy entrapment: MY DOOMSDAY!

In the nick of time, somebody up there came and pulled me back. God pulled me back. I felt that somebody really cared for me. I just knew the balm of forgiveness because of my relationship with God.

I saw hope. I knew there was hope for me. Oh, folks, I just broke down and wept like a baby. Something was working into my sensibilities: the mighty hand of my Creator— invisible, yet INVINCIBLE! I gave him glory. He gave me victory. I stood six feet tall.

If you ask me now about my conviction as to motivation, I declare based on the facts that I stood by my faith until my last gasp of a flickering and forlorn hope.

Let us be strong, with faith in our beliefs.

This is a wake-up call to all and every person living in the United States of America.

Let us look back at that eaglet which fell to the ground a number of times, but each fall made its wings stronger because that eaglet never gave up.

Ladies and gentlemen, we, too, can realize our visions and dreams so long as, like that eaglet in the spirit of freedom, we keep trying and never give up.

Yes, let us get away from our bootstraps, to the limitless opportunities, unto the sky. Come fly with me.

Exclusive Copyright@2012 by PACQUIAO UNDER CROSSFIRE
for Lorne Scoggins, Forth Smith Boxing Examiner; Taken by the ringside during Pacquiao-Margarito fight at the Dallas Cowboy Stadium in Arlington, Texas on November 13, 2010.

The Woman behind the Author's Success

"Every adversity, every failure, and every heartache, carries with it the seed of an equivalent or greater benefit." - Napoleon Hill

***Exclusive photo copyright @ 2012 by* PACQUIAO UNDER CROSSFIRE**
for Maria Almita Moleta-Bonifacio

Pacquiao Under Crossfire

*P*ACQUIAO UNDER CROSSFIRE is a very interesting book in a different kind of format that will make readers curious about the subject matter. It is a great tribute to not only the boxing star, but to boxing in general. The author's creative skill makes the book exciting even for people who do not follow boxing or have not been interested in it before seeing this book.

-Xulon Press

Praises for C.S. Granville from Fellow Credentialed Journalists

"Granville Ampong has opened a new frontier in "sports writing." His unique style, backed up by his passion to be good and yet different, separates him from the pack."
— Ed de la Vega, Graduate of the University of Southern California School of Dentistry; Restorative, Cosmetic and Sports Dentistry. Part-time boxing writer and photo-journalist; Multi-state licensed boxing & MMA cut-man and maker of custom-designed World Mouthguards

"Granville Ampong is like a baseball umpire who calls them as he uniquely sees them. If the pitch is down the middle, this writer calls it a strike. If it is high and wide, off the mark, he says so in plain language. Ampong admires the Great Man Pacquiao, yes, but he is no idol worshipper. If you want fluff and rump-kissing, look elsewhere. Ampong serves up his views and observations straight, no chaser. He is always a good, informative read."
— Michael Marley, Law Offices of Attorney Michael Marley, New York

"Granville Ampong brings an honesty in his writings on Manny Pacquiao, conqueror of the American heartlands. The author has always seen the Filipino hero with a clarity which says as much about the writer, as it does the fighter. It is a chapter in history which in later years will be remembered as ground-breaking. These essays will form a part of that history."
   — **Gareth A Davies, The Telegraph - London, United Kingdom**

"Granville Ampong's passion and dedication to the sport of boxing are easily recognized in the tone of his work. While the true journalism and pure objectivism that he demonstrates invite both acclaim and criticism, he continues to report the truth, and only the truth, exactly as he sees it."
   —**Lorne Scoggins, Fort Smith Boxing Examiner and Associate Pastor of Christian Lighthouse Church in Springdale, Arkansas**

"Granville Ampong's book is a great collection of stories that vividly captivate the man that has become the Philippines' national treasure. His words meant no patronizing, yet he elevated the boxing champ into a high pedestal. He captured snapshots of the People's Champ and transformed them into enthralling narratives. This book is a total knockout!"
   — **Robbie Pangilinan, Founder of SportsManila.net**

"Recent books about Manny Pacquiao explore the topic of his life, his real needs, struggles, fears, desires. But it was Granville who ventured into this terrain with his revolutionary book. Now, with the new material from the author that relates the book's classic message to today's struggling professional boxers, PACQUIAO UNDER CROSSFIRE continues to tell the truth. It reveals what every struggling professional boxer needs to know about Manny Pacquiao and his conquests. And what every struggling boxer needs to know about himself. A syndicated columnist at Western Center for Journalism, Granville has written a refreshing and readable account of the complexities of being a celebrity and world champion at the same time. Aside from the vivid examples and lively prose, what makes Granville's book particularly engaging is that the author makes linguistics interesting and usable. This book could be the Rosetta Stone that at last deciphers the misconceptions about Manny Pacquiao as a politician, actor, world champion rolled into one."

—**Alex P. Vidal, New Millennium Publication, Philippines**

"Reading Granville Ampong's work is like having a hot cup of coffee with him sitting across you and speaking his mind on issues close to his heart with eclectic inputs not limited to the temporal but also the spiritual realm. He writes as he talks so leafing through the pages of his book is akin to engaging him in good conversation. His works are good material for those seeking to delve deeper into the myriad issues in the world of boxing."

—**Alex Rey Pal, Dumaguete MetroPost, Philippines**

CPSIA information can be obtained at www.ICGtesting.com
Printed in the USA
BVOW012233131112
305498BV00001B/10/P